Echoes of American Ballet

ECHOES OF AMERICAN BALLET

A Collection of Seventeen Articles Written and

Selected by LILLIAN MOORE

Edited, and with an Introduction

by IVOR GUEST

Dance Horizons • New York • 1976

International Standard Book Number 0-87127-064-1

Library of Congress Catalog Card Number 75-9160

Printed in the United States of America

Dance Horizons, 1801 East 26th Street
Brooklyn, New York 11229

Acknowledgments

Our thanks to the following for permission to
reprint articles which originally appeared in their
publications: *Dance Index, Dance Magazine,
Dancing Times,* The New York Public Library
(Bulletin of The New York Public Library),
Theodore Presser Co. *(Etude),* The Theatre Guild
(Theatre Guild Magazine), W.C.C. Publishing Co.,
Inc. *(New York Herald Tribune).*
We wish to acknowledge our sincere appreciation to
the Dance Collection and Music and Rare Book
Divisions of The New York Public Library, the
Harvard Theatre Collection, the Collections of the
Historical Society of York County, Pennsylvania;
Allison Delarue and Louis Péres for permission to
use illustrative material from their collections; also to
Mr. Péres, Martha Swope and Asgar Sessingø for
the use of their photographs. Frank Derbas and Mr.
Péres were especially helpful in making the
necessary photographic copies of rare material.
Our special thanks go to Barbara Cohen who did
the research for the illustrations and compiled
the index.

Contents

Illustrations

Lillian Moore, Copenhagen, 1961

Introduction by Ivor Guest:
The Legacy of Lillian Moore

D ANCE HISTORIANS of the calibre of Lillian Moore are so exceedingly rare that it was a tragedy for scholarship that she should die in the prime of her life and with so many projects unfulfilled. The dance world faced a double sacrifice: the loss not only of an authoritative writer and critic, but also of the great history of the theatrical dance in America which she had been planning in the all too few intervals of her busy life. This should have been the monument by which she would be remembered. The articles collected in this volume cover a few of the highlights that would have illumined the definitive study that was awaited from her pen, but being written as isolated contributions to various periodicals, they give no idea of the shape she planned for her history. Perhaps it is just as well that we are not vouchsafed an insight into the extent of our deprivation.

No one could have been better qualified than Lillian Moore to undertake the task of chronicling the story of theatrical dancing in America from Colonial and Revolutionary times to the splendid achievements of today. Historical research for her was an all-absorbing passion, and she was seldom happier than when the clues she was following up led her into new corridors of knowledge. No details were too unimportant to ignore, and she would go to endless trouble in ferreting out hitherto unknown facts to fill some empty space in the jigsaw of her project. With her burning determination and inexhaustible patience, and, equally important, the uncanny insight which directed her research, went an infectious enthusiasm that shines still through her words on the printed page. Added to these qualities was a strong pride in being American, a deep love for her country and a wide knowledge of its history and traditions—qualities that most admirably fitted her, a professional dancer and dance teacher, for what she must have forseen, in ignorance of the cruel dictates of her fate, as the crowning achievement of her career.

She was a true child of the New World. Born in Chase City, a small town in Virginia, on September 20, 1911, she gravitated early to New York, which became her permanent home. There, at the old Metropolitan Opera, she made her first stage appearance as a dancer and her first solo appearance at the age of nineteen in Rossini's opera *William Tell*. The flowering of American ballet which began with the arrival of Balanchine and the establishment of the School of American Ballet was only a few years in the future, and it was in the stimulating atmosphere of the nineteen-thirties, when the dance was establishing itself in American cultural life, that she matured both as an artist and as a writer.

From 1935 to 1938 she danced with the American Ballet, founded by Lincoln Kirstein and Balanchine; in 1938 she gave her own New York concert in the McMillin Theater at Columbia University; between 1938 and 1941 she was a soloist at the Metropolitan Opera under Boris Romanov; and in 1940 she gained the recognition of Fokine who engaged her as a guest artist for the Fokine Ballet. During the war years she was ballet-mistress and prima ballerina with the Cincinnati Summer Opera Company, and in 1945-46 she toured the Pacific theatre with the U.S.O. Jerome Kern Show. After the war she visited Europe to give performances for the American troops, and in Budapest in November 1948 she had the honour of being the first American dancer to appear behind the Iron Curtain. In the early 1950s she toured the States in a programme of character and satirical dances of her own devising.

She retired as a performer in 1954 to devote herself to teaching and writing. By then she had already gained an international reputation as an historian; her first article (reprinted here as No. XI) had been published in 1929 and this had been followed by regular contributions to the dance magazines of New York and London. In 1938, in the midst of an active life as a performer, she brought out her first book, *Artists of the Dance*, a survey of the lives and careers of a succession of great dancers from Camargo to Balanchine and Martha Graham. It was an important contribution to dance literature, remarkable for its accuracy and containing new material based on her personal research. While her research touched many periods and many centres, it was the American scene that held her in special thrall and the five monographs she contributed to the scholarly periodical, *Dance Index*, were all concerned with the dance in the Western hemisphere: *The Petipa Family in Europe and America* (May 1942, and here reprinted as No. X), *John Durang, the First American Dancer* (August 1942), *Mary Ann Lee, First American Giselle* (May 1943) and *George Washington Smith* (June-August 1945) are standard source works for the history of dancing in the United States, while in the fifth, *Moreau de Saint-Méry and "Danse"* (October 1946), she was inspired by an old book, published in Philadelphia shortly after the Revolution, to enquire into the native dances of Haiti.

It was about this time that our paths crossed — if that expression can be used to describe an exchange of letters between Germany, where I was serving in the British army, and Hawaii, where she was dancing for the troops. I had written to tell her of the enjoyment which her article on Giuseppina Bozzacchi, the first Swanilda in *Coppélia*, had given me, and had almost despaired of a reply when a warm and generous letter reached me after a journey half way round the world. From then on we corresponded regularly, confiding our plans for future projects and exchanging information about the discoveries we were making in our researches. Re-reading her letters I realise what a close communion of minds we achieved. Separated by the Atlantic, we saw each other all too infrequently, sometimes in London, and later in New York, and my memories of those rare meetings are now doubly precious. Her apartment at 406 West 46th Street, which she shared with her husband, David Maclay, a Division Chief of The New York Public Library, and two or three adored and very spoilt cats, was a veritable museum of the dance, and I recall with nostalgia the happy hours I spent there looking at her treasure trove of books, prints, statuettes and other memorabilia of the dance. Her collection was all the more remarkable for being built up with her hard-earned savings, and often at very considerable sacrifice. The possession of which she was proudest of all was a portrait of Fanny Elssler — a favourite ballerina we shared — and her son, painted on ivory, which was so expensive that she had to pay for it by instalments spread over many months. By any standards it was the find of a collector's lifetime, and she generously allowed me to use it to illustrate my biography of Elssler. Today it is in the Theatre Collection of Harvard College Library, to whom she bequeathed it by her will. The bulk of her collection she left to the Dance Collection of The New York Public Library. It is a satisfaction to know that her treasures have been preserved for scholars and students for all time.

The tempo of her life did not slacken after her retirement as a performer. She was a member of the faculty of the High School of Performing Arts from 1950 to 1958, and the following year she joined the faculty of Robert Joffrey's American Ballet Center to direct the apprentice and scholarship programme. She also served on the President's Advisory Commission on the Arts and on the dance evaluation panel of the New York State Arts Council. In spite of these time-consuming commitments she still found time to do research and write, and the last thirteen years of her life saw the publication of five important works, in addition to many articles for dance magazines (she was New York correspondent of the

Dancing Times to the time of her death), a multitude of entries on ballet and dancers for the monumental *Enciclopedia dello Spettacolo*, of which she was one of the advisers on ballet, and an annual survey of ballet for the *Encyclopedia Brittanica* Book of the Year.

All five of these major works filled gaps in dance literature, and taken together they reveal the breadth of her inquiring mind. They began, in 1958, with *Russian Ballet Master*, the first English translation, by Helen Whittaker, of the memoirs of Marius Petipa, which Lillian edited. Then came a more substantial work which was very close to her heart, *Bournonville and Ballet Technique* (1961), which she wrote in collaboration with the great Danish dancer, Erik Bruhn. The Bournonville heritage, so carefully preserved at the Royal Theatre in Copenhagen, held a special meaning for her both as dancer and as historian, and she seldom allowed a European trip to pass without visiting the charming Danish capital to see the Bournonville ballets performed in their original setting and to work in the Royal Library where she made some exciting discoveries. It is in libraries that the creative energies of a theatre historian are nourished and Lillian had a second home in the famous Dance Collection of The New York Public Library. The commission, therefore, to write a historical survey of the dance around the many pictures and prints in the Collection gave her great satisfaction, and the splendidly produced volume that emerged—*Images of the Dance* (1965)—is as much a pleasure to read and to handle, as it must have been to write. There remain the two monographs she contributed to the periodical, *Dance Perspectives*. Of all her works, I feel that the one which afforded her the most delight was *The Duport Mystery* (1960), for it was the product of a long period of successful sleuthing in a field untouched by other researchers and much of its narrative was set in Philadelphia and Charleston towards the end of the eighteenth century. The second of these monographs was *Prints on Pushcarts* (1962), a catalogue of the dance prints of Currier and Ives with an introduction that breathes Lillian's involvement with her subject.

During the last fifteen years of her life, in such intervals as she could spare between her many commitments, Lillian was gathering material for her great history of the theatrical dance in America. The task was formidable, but the start of the work was assisted by a grant from the Rockefeller Foundation. Anxious to see the book materialise on my shelves, I seldom wrote to her without enquiring about its progress. But it was clear that she intended to take her time, to cover the ground thoroughly. "My 'American' research progresses with painful slowness," she told me in November 1956, "and I will be able to include only about a tenth of the material I have gathered, in the book, but at least I will have data at hand for dozens of articles and perhaps even further books. There are so many unsolved problems, and I hate to publish the book without clearing them up." Two months later she confessed that she was "feeling very discouraged about my book and all phases of my research," because a multitude of "writing chores" were preventing her from doing "really concentrated work." In May 1957, "research on the book has been put aside for about six weeks, ever since I started to work intensely on the Brittanica piece." That year her interest in Louis Duport (which was to bear fruit in *The Duport Mystery*) "quite side-tracked me from my early American research." A letter of July 1958 told me: "My American research has suffered from the Petipa diversion, and various other things, but I keep plodding along." And so, with interruptions caused by her many other activities, the process of gathering material continued fitfully, and alas, the stage of putting pen to paper had not arrived when Lillian's last illness supervened.

It was typical of her to conceal the gravity of her condition. It was only to excuse her delay in reviewing a book of mine that she mentioned that she had undergone a "minor operation" in the fall of 1966. "Now I just want to forget all about it!" she wrote. "My parents do not even know that I was in the hospital at all, or that I was ill—I just missed going out to Stamford to see them, for one week-end; and most of my friends here don't know it either." In the summer of 1967 she became desperately ill, and on July 28th she died of cancer at the Flower and Fifth Avenue Hospitals, New York.

With her death the dance world lost one of its finest historians. How will the importance of her life's work be judged? There are her works, an impressive series of studies. But also there is the example of scholarship which she set, an example which has inspired, and will continue to inspire, many other writers of her own and later generations. Before her time the writing of dance history was, with few exceptions, a casual, often amateur, affair; there were great uncharted gaps which writers ignored as if those years had not existed, and errors would be slavishly copied from book to book for want of effort to check facts. Lillian showed that this was not good enough. By the method and depth of her research work she helped to set new standards in the writing of dance history. Her style was so easy and alive that the long hours she must have spent in libraries gathering facts and background from books, newspapers, manuscripts and prints can easily be overlooked, and in a study of her work as a historian it is necessary to emphasise the preliminary process of research which, because she never skimped, gave her writings a foundation of real scholarship. Analyse every article in this collection and it will be found that they all throw new light on some aspect of the history of the dance.

These articles were, as will be seen from the details of their first publication, written over a period of thirty-four years and for periodicals appealing to different readerships. A different style is called for when writing for a daily newspaper than for contributing to a specialist dance magazine. So I make no apology for variations in approach. Undoubtedly, if Lillian herself had been preparing these essays for publication, she would have made revisions and additions to give the collection cohesion, but this is beyond the scope of an editor's task and I have therefore limited my editing to the removal of certain topical allusions which were appropriate when the article was first written but have now lost their force, and a few factual corrections made necessary by recent research. In the Petipa article, for example, I have been able to include the correct date of Marius Petipa's birth which was recently discovered during the preparations for the commemorative volume on the great choreographer published in Russia in 1971.

I also make no apology for including the articles on Dupré and Henriette Hendel, which have only an indirect relevance to the American scene. Not only did they seem to me too valuable to be discarded, but it was the wish of Lillian herself that they should be reprinted in this collection.

When I was asked to edit these articles, I remembered how generous Lillian was in sharing the results of her research with others and I felt she would have been satisfied to know that these casual pieces were being made available to students and scholars in a more permanent form. Maybe indeed someone reading her words will be moved to take up the task of compiling that great history of the theatrical dance in America. These pages, therefore, are offered not only as a memorial to a great historian and a dear friend, but as an inspiration to others whose imagination may be stirred, as hers was, to recreate the struggles, the glories and the heartaches of times past.

Echoes of American Ballet

I: The International Ballet Heritage

MANY BOOKS have been written about ballet technique and tradition, but it is through the direct personal contact of teacher and pupil that the art has really been preserved and developed. Each great artist, in transmitting the ballet heritage to his students, has incorporated his discoveries and those of other dancers of his generation, so that the body of knowledge has gradually expanded. A lesson given today by George Balanchine or Vera Volkova would undoubtedly include many things unknown to Louis Dupré, yet there is no doubt that their methods are still firmly based on the principles he employed.

The heritage of any well-schooled ballet dancer can be traced straight back to the beginning of the eighteenth century, through the teachers of his teachers. Here we have partially explored (partially, because any dancer of international calibre has of course been trained by more than two teachers) the artistic ancestry of three of the greatest dancers of our time. Each is generally conceded to be an outstanding example of the ballet in her own country: Fonteyn, of England; Ulanova, of Soviet Russia; and Tallchief, of America.

Nevertheless, the three have "ancestors" in common, just one or two generations back. Each of them has, also, several distinct "lines," through which the influence of the French, Russian and Italian schools can be distinctly seen. In each case, too, it is just eight steps (by the most direct line) back to the great Louis Dupré, star of the Paris Opéra in the brilliant days of Marie Camargo and Marie Sallé.

Dupré himself has been almost totally forgotten (it was not until we started to trace these dance "genealogies" that we actually realized that he taught the three great figures of late eighteenth-century ballet, Gardel, Vestris, and Noverre) but his contemporaries were extravagant in praise of his lightness, grace, and nobility of style. Jacques Casanova devoted a long passage in his famed memoirs to Dupré's wonderful dancing.

If you are a dancer, you can probably trace your own "ancestors" back to this same source. The first few steps may be different (for example, in my own case I can trace one line through my very first teacher, Gertrude Colburn, to Elisabetta Menzelli to Paul Taglioni to Filippo Taglioni to Pierre Gardel), but fairly soon you are sure to get back to one of the great figures like Cecchetti or Legat or Johansson. It is a simple way to grasp the richness of the common heritage shared by ballet dancers all over the world.

—*Dance Magazine*, January 1958

Galina Ulanova. (Martha Swope)

GALINA ULANOVA

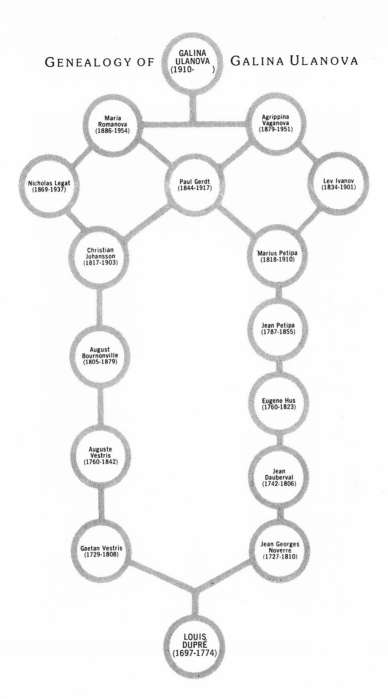

Maria Tallchief. (Martha Swope)

GENEALOGY OF MARIA TALLCHIEF

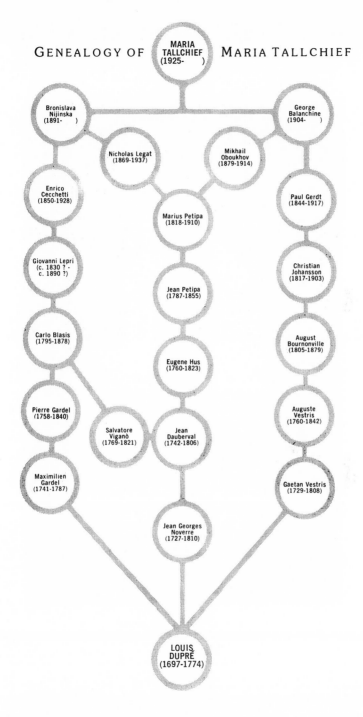

MARIA TALLCHIEF (1925-)

Bronislava Nijinska (1891-)

George Balanchine (1904-)

Nicholas Legat (1869-1937)

Mikhail Oboukhov (1879-1914)

Enrico Cecchetti (1850-1928)

Paul Gerdt (1844-1917)

Marius Petipa (1818-1910)

Giovanni Lepri (c. 1830 ? - c. 1890 ?)

Christian Johansson (1817-1903)

Jean Petipa (1787-1855)

Carlo Blasis (1795-1878)

August Bournonville (1805-1879)

Eugene Hus (1760-1823)

Pierre Gardel (1758-1840)

Salvatore Viganò (1769-1821)

Jean Dauberval (1742-1806)

Auguste Vestris (1760-1842)

Maximilien Gardel (1741-1787)

Gaetan Vestris (1729-1808)

Jean Georges Noverre (1727-1810)

LOUIS DUPRÉ (1697-1774)

15

Margot Fonteyn. (Louis Péres)

MARGOT FONTEYN

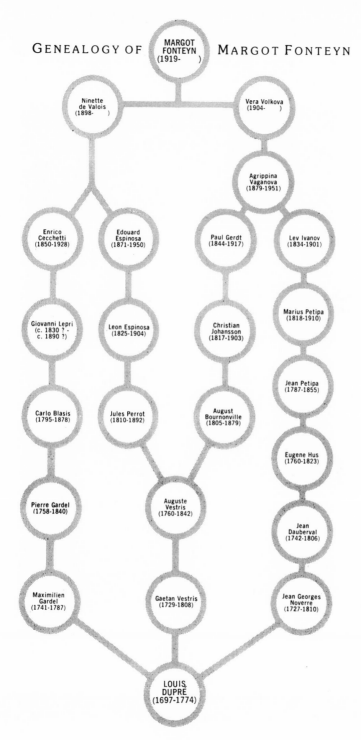

MARGOT FONTEYN (1919-   )

Ninette de Valois (1898-   )

Vera Volkova (1904-   )

Agrippina Vaganova (1879-1951)

Enrico Cecchetti (1850-1928)

Edouard Espinosa (1871-1950)

Paul Gerdt (1844-1917)

Lev Ivanov (1834-1901)

Giovanni Lepri (c. 1830 ? - c. 1890 ?)

Leon Espinosa (1825-1904)

Christian Johansson (1817-1903)

Marius Petipa (1818-1910)

Jean Petipa (1787-1855)

Carlo Blasis (1795-1878)

Jules Perrot (1810-1892)

August Bournonville (1805-1879)

Eugene Hus (1760-1823)

Pierre Gardel (1758-1840)

Auguste Vestris (1760-1842)

Jean Dauberval (1742-1806)

Maximilien Gardel (1741-1787)

Gaetan Vestris (1729-1808)

Jean Georges Noverre (1727-1810)

LOUIS DUPRÉ (1697-1774)

17

Although there is no portrait of Dupré, this costume for Apollo was designed for a Paris Opéra production by contemporary Jean Baptiste Martin. The chances are excellent that it suggests the style and manner of Dupré. (Dance Collection, The New York Public Library)

II: The Great Dupré

LOUIS DUPRÉ was the prototype of the *premier danseur noble*. Although he is mentioned, casually, in almost every history of ballet, his glamorous contemporaries, Camargo and Sallé, seem to have commanded the attention of recent writers so effectively that his enormous contribution has not received proper attention.

It was while working on the "dance genealogies" of Margot Fonteyn, Maria Tallchief and Galina Ulanova that I first became conscious of the tremendous importance of Dupré, for every line of descent, from teacher to pupil, seemed to lead right back to him, the great-great-great-great-great grandfather of them all. He was the teacher of three of the most vital figures in eighteenth-century ballet — Maximilian Gardel, Gaetan Vestris and Jean Georges Noverre. Through their pupils, his influence has extended through the French, Russian and Italian schools, down to the present day.

Almost every contemporary mention of Louis Dupré refers to him as "*le grand Dupré*." The word *grand* was used in a double sense, to indicate his artistic importance, and, meaning "tall," in tribute to his stature. Although he lacked being six feet tall by two inches, he apparently towered over his fellow dancers in a century when men were admittedly smaller than they are today. The epithet "*le grand Dupré*" also distinguished him from another dancer, the shorter and less talented Jean-Denis Dupré, known as "*le petit*."

The two Duprés may have been brothers. Jean-Denis, born in Paris in 1706, was the son of a dancing master named Jean Dupré. Louis, born about 1697, was probably the little Dupré who appeared at the Paris Opéra in children's roles, in *Scylla* in 1701, *Phaeton* in 1702, and as Cupid in *Ulysse* in 1703. In view of the magnificent technique for which he was famous later on, and which must have been acquired at an early age, this seems more probable than the widely repeated legend that he was a violinist in the theatre orchestra at Rouen before he became a dancer.

Dupré studied under Louis Pécourt, distinguished choreographer at the Paris Opéra, and made his formal debut there in 1714, dancing a pas de deux with Mlle. Guyot in *Télémaque*. Although the older, established dancers Jean Ballon and Michel Blondy claimed the most prominent roles, the young Dupré was soon acclaimed for the elegance, grace and purity of his style. He appeared in many of the opera-ballets of Jean Baptiste Lully, such as *Amadis, Acis et Galatée*, and *Thésée*.

Dissatisfied with his limited opportunities at the Opéra, Dupré took advantage of his annual vacations to appear in other countries. In London, in 1717, he participated in a notable experiment, the production of John Weaver's ballet pantomime *The Loves of Mars and Venus*, at Drury Lane Theatre. This performance, a milestone in the development of dramatic ballet, was one of the earliest attempts, since ancient times, to tell a story through dancing alone. Louis Dupré danced the role of Mars, with Hester Santlow, an English girl whom Weaver called "the Wonder and Admiration of the present Age," as Venus. The choreographer himself played Vulcan. Part of the action of the principals is quaintly described in Weaver's rare libretto:

> Scene IV—A Garden.
> . . . Mars with his Followers enter on one Side; and Venus, with Graces, etc., on the other. Mars and Venus meet and embrace; Gallantry, Respect; Ardent Love; and Adoration; appear in the actions of Mars: An affected Bashfulness; reciprocal Love; and wishing Looks, in Venus; they sit on a Couch, while the four Followers of Mars begin the Entry; to whom the Graces joyn; and afterwards Mars and Venus: at which time Cupid steals away the Arms of Mars and his Followers . . .

In spite of his contribution to this pioneer pantomimic ballet, produced before Jean Georges Noverre was born, Dupré was by inclination and temperament a classical, rather than a dramatic dancer. Much later, in his famous *Lettres sur la Danse*, Noverre was to rail at him for always dancing *chaconnes* and *passacailles*, in which he excelled, instead of varying his style of dancing to suit the theme of the ballet.

It was the technical brilliance of such dancers as Dupré and Camargo which had made dancing for its own sake sufficiently spectacular to hold the interest of the public. This was anathema to Noverre, who thought that dancing without dramatic motivation was meaningless and empty. Nevertheless, he was too sincere an artist not to recognize superior merit, even when it shone in an alien field, and he had a deep respect and admiration for the man who was his teacher.

"Big open movements of the leg and *éffacé* positions were without doubt suited to M. Dupré," wrote Noverre, "the elegance of his figure and the length of his limbs were wonderfully suited to the execution of *développés éffacés* and the intricate steps of the dance . . . This rare harmony in every movement earned for the celebrated Dupré the glorious title of *Dieu de la Danse*: and in fact this excellent dancer seemed a divinity rather than a man: the calm and flowing continuity of his every movement and the perfect coordination and control of every muscle made for a perfect ensemble due to a fine physique, precise arrangement and well-combined proportion of every part and which, resulting less from study and reasoning than from nature, may only be acquired when one is so endowed . . ."

Dupré was apparently the first to be called *le dieu de la danse*, a title inherited by his pupils, Gaetan Vestris, and later by Vestris' son Auguste. At the height of his career, an anonymous poet rhapsodized:

> Ah! que je vois Dupré qui s'avance:
> Comme il développe ses bras!
> Que des grâces dans tous ses pas!
> C'est ma foi le Dieu de la Danse.
> (Ah! I see Dupré advance:
> How he slowly opens his arms!
> What grace in his every step!
> In faith, it is the God of the Dance.)

In 1722, Dupré left the Paris Opéra to dance abroad. In 1725 he was in London, where apparently he had a school, for he presented some of his pupils at the theatre in Lincoln's Inn Fields. He also danced in Dresden, and spent a considerable time in Poland. When Michel Blondy retired from dancing to assume the post of *maître de ballet* at the Paris Opéra, in 1730, Dupré returned to France to replace him as *premier danseur*.

Dupré made his reappearance on November 12, 1730, in *Thésée*. Soon he was the favorite partner of Marie Sallé, whose gracious and noble style admirably complemented his own. Their names were linked in a *bon mot* which went the rounds of Paris society. It listed the four marvels of the Opéra as the voice of Mlle. Lemaure, the legs of Mlle. Mariette, Dupré's marvellous elasticity of movement, and the virtue of Mlle. Sallé.

In spite of the aristocratic elegance of his dancing, and his later distinction as a teacher, Louis Dupré seems to have been practically illiterate. In 1732, things were not going smoothly between the artists of the Paris Opéra and the director, Lecomte. Dupré had signed a contract in December, 1730, and it had been ratified eight months later. Nevertheless, in March, 1732, he appeared before a Paris magistrate and filed a legal complaint that Lecomte had forced him, under false pretenses, to sign *"un papier tout ecrit"* (a paper all written out) without having had it read aloud to him first; he feared that he had unwittingly agreed to a new and less favorable contract, and before it could go into effect he wished to record his ignorance of its contents and the fact that it had been signed under duress!

Well, at least he could sign his name; and it is a regrettable fact that illiteracy was so generally prevalent, in the early eighteenth century, that many otherwise capable people could not even do that!

His namesake, *"le petit"* Dupré (Jean-Denis), was anything but illiterate. Although he was not a particularly distinguished dancer, he was an expert at the Feuillet system of dance notation. According to Noverre, the famous teacher Marcel made fun of Jean-Denis Dupré's dependence on notation, calling him "an imbecile choreographer and a poor master who dances paper in hand." At any rate, Jean-Denis was probably the Dupré who published a treatise on dancing (now extremely rare) at Mans, France, in 1757, under the cumbersome title of *Méthode trés facile et fort nécessaire, pour apprendre soi-même la chorégraphie ou l'art d'écrire et de déchiffrer les danse.*

Louis Dupré apparently resolved his difficulties with the management of the Paris Opéra, for he remained one of its brightest stars for twenty more years. He partnered Camargo, as well as Sallé. The list of his roles runs literally into the hundreds, but he very seldom had a dramatic part; usually he danced in divertissements, and was listed as "a faun," "a shepherd," "a Roman," or "a Pleasure." Although dignity and grace were among his highest assets, he seems to have enjoyed dancing grotesque demons and furies, too, and the *Dictionnaire Encyclopédique* records the fact that, in such roles, he executed brilliant *gargouillades*, although with less elevation than his successors, Gaetan and Auguste Vestris, gave them. Cahusac, writing after Dupré's retirement, declared that no man ever had a finer physique, danced with more elegance, or assumed classic ballet positions with greater nobility and ease.

The mask was still in general use among male dancers at the Paris Opéra throughout Dupré's career. If he had any outstanding ability as a dance-actor, which is doubtful, the mask would have hidden his feature from the audience anyway.

In 1739, on the death of Blondy, Dupré was appointed *maître de ballet* of the Paris Opéra, for which he staged many ballet divertissements. Carlo Blasis has revealed one of the methods by which Dupré trained himself to be a choreographer. Writing in 1820, in his *Traité Elémentaire,*

Théorique et Pratique de la Danse, he said: "To hasten their progress in dance composition, why do not our young dancers follow the example of Dupré? This artist used to improvise to unfamiliar music, in order to develop his imagination in inventing steps and *enchaînements*, and to accustom his ear to grasp promptly the rhythm and phrasing of the music . . ." Blasis also deplored the fact that although character and comedy dancing had advanced, the *genre serieux*, or classic style, had declined since the days of Dupré and the elder Vestris.

Louis Dupré also staged dance for the Opéra Comique at the Foire Saint-Laurent, and in this capacity, in the summer of 1743, he gave the sixteen-year-old Jean Georges Noverre his first professional job.

According to Noverre, Dupré was outwardly cold and phlegmatic, but was passionately fond of hunting, women, and flowers. Noverre, coming for a lesson, often found him in a bad humor, so he frequently tried to soften his temper by bringing him a bouquet. He also entertained Dupré by dancing a rondo taught him by Marcel, under rather unusual circumstances.

Noverre had called on Marcel and found him completely incapacitated by gout. Noverre, determined to have a lesson anyway, asked the old man to indicate the movements with his fingers. In this way Noverre learned a rondo in the ancient style, which he promptly showed to Dupré. Thereafter, whenever Dupré was grouchy, Noverre would restore his good humor by dancing Marcel's old-fashioned rondo.

For many years Dupré headed the school of dancing at the Paris Opéra, and there he formed such distinguished dancers as Maximilien Gardel and Gaetan Vestris. One of his favorite pupils was Marianne Cochois, later a rival of Barberina Campanini at the court of Frederick the Great. When he first saw her dance, he claimed that in six months he could make her the finest dancer who had ever appeared at the Opéra. Perhaps he might have succeeded (in year, if not months) if she had not deserted Paris for Berlin.

Touchard-Lafosse, writing about a century later, claimed that it was Dupré who first established the teaching of ballet as a real art, thanks to his precise understanding of ballet technique, and his unique ability to demonstrate each step and movement with exquisite perfection. Touchard-Lafosse also said that the divertissements staged by Dupré, which (although they employed characters from Greek mythology) were usually plotless and more or less "abstract" in design, contained more poetry than the forced efforts of many pretentious writers who claimed to be poets.

Dupré also taught social dances (the minuet was then much in favor) to

members of the nobility; and one of his aristocratic pupils, M. de Cour-
tanvaux, became so proficient an amateur ballet dancer that he was able
to win the favor of King Louis XV, as *premier danseur* of his private
theatre at Versailles.

Dupré danced with undiminished success until he was over fifty. In
1751 he was granted an annual pension of 1,500 Livres, which continued until his death in December, 1774. He remained an active
member of the exclusive and influential Académie Royale de Danse,
which admitted only thirteen members (including also the lesser Dupré,
Jean-Denis).

At Fontainebleau, in November 1752, Dupré danced a minuet with
Marie Sallé in a private performance of *l'Inconnu*, before the Court. This
was probably his farewell performance. Dufort de Cheverny, who attended it, called him "majestic" but "lacking in strength." On the other
hand, Giovanni Gallini, a Paris Opéra dancer who became an important
theatre manager in London, wrote of his last performance: "I have myself
seen the celebrated Dupré, at near the age of sixty, dance at Paris with all
the agility and sprightliness of youth, and with such a power of pleasing as
if the graces in him had braved super-annuation."

Jacques Casanova, who saw him dance in *Les Fêtes Venitiennes* in
1750, has left the most famous (and perhaps the most vivid) description
of Dupré:

> The action depicted a day during the carnival, a time when the Venetians are
> accustomed to promenading, masked, in St. Mark's square . . . The costumes
> were bizarre and inaccurate, but the whole scene was amusing. It made me laugh,
> and indeed for a Venetian it was very funny to see the Doge and twelve
> counsellors, all in exotic costumes, come out of the wings and begin to dance a
> *passacaille*. Suddenly I heard everyone clapping at the appearance of a tall,
> fine-looking masked dancer, wearing an enormous black wig which reached
> half-way to his waist, and dressed in a costume, open in front, which fell to his
> heels. Patu (*this was the friend with whom Casanova had attended the perform-
> ance*) told me, with a sort of veneration: "It is the inimitable Dupré." I had heard
> of him, and watched attentively.
>
> I see a handsome figure advancing with measured steps; reaching the front of
> the stage, he moves his feet with lightness and precision, extending and withdraw-
> ing them, does some little steps, a few *battements* at the calf, a *pirouette*, and then
> disappears like a zephyr. The whole thing had not lasted half a minute. Applause
> and bravos broke out from every part of the house; I was astonished, and asked
> my friend the reason.
>
> "They applaud the grace of Dupré, and the divine harmony of his movements.
> He is sixty years old, and those who saw him forty years ago find him still the
> same."
>
> "What? He has never danced differently?"

"He could not have danced better, for what you have seen him do is perfect, and what is beyond perfection?"

"Nothing; at least, unless perfection is relative."

"Here it is absolute. Dupré has always done the same thing, and each day we believe we are seeing it for the first time. Such is the power of the beautiful and the good, the sublime and the true, which penetrates the soul. This dance is a harmony; it is the real dance, of which you in Italy have no idea."

At the end of the second act, there was Dupré again, his face covered by a mask, dancing to different music, but to my eyes, doing the same thing. He came forward to the very front of the stage, then stopped for a moment in a perfectly designed position. Patu wanted me to admire him; I obliged. Suddenly I heard a hundred voices from the audience, saying: *"Ah, mon Dieu! mon Dieu! Il se développe, il se développe!"* Actually, his seemed an elastic body which, when he did a *développé*, became taller. I made Patu happy by telling him that it was true that Dupré had perfect grace.

—*Dance Magazine*, June 1960

Henriette Hendel. From *Pantomimische Stellungen von Henriette Hendel* by Joseph Nicolaus Peroux. (Dance Collection, The New York Public Library)

III: Eighteenth Century Isadora: Henriette Hendel

LIKE ISADORA DUNCAN, she found her inspiration in the art of ancient Greece. Like Ruth St. Denis, she experimented in the imaginative use of lighting and drapery. Like Angna Enters, she found themes in the Madonnas of Flemish and Italian painters. Again like Isadora, she led a full and highly unconventional life, in which love was as important as her art. Poets celebrated her, and even Goethe paid her tribute. Nevertheless, the name of Henriette Hendel has disappeared into all but complete oblivion.

Hendel lived a whole century ahead of her time, and her experiments and innovations were so startlingly new that her contemporaries in the professional theatre were quite unable to grasp their significance. Admired and appreciated as an individual artist, Hendel enjoyed a personal success which lasted for many years, but the actors, dancers and choreographers of her time never succeeded in applying her theories on a broader scale, and she had no permanent influence on either the interpretation of the spoken drama or the theatrical dance.

In an age when divorce was so rare that it could cause the social ostracism of a woman who risked it, Henriette Hendel was married no less than four times. In 1811, a friend wrote to Goethe that he had just seen "Madame Schütz, formerly Hendel, fore-formerly Meyer, fore-fore-formerly Eunicke, née Schüler."

The adventurous life of Johanne Henriette Rosine Schüler began in Döbeln, in the Saxon part of Germany, on February 13, 1772. Her parents were actors, and they were on the way from Breslau to Gotha, where the father had an engagement, when the baby was born. The little family was able to remain in Döbeln only a few days before hurrying on, and during the cold, snowy journey the tiny girl nearly died.

Little Henriette was literally raised on the stage. At the age of two, she was carried on for a scene requiring an infant, and embarrassed her father by struggling out of his arms and toddling forward, singing and dancing happily, when she recognized the occupant of the prompter's box, a close friend of the family. At four, the precocious youngster received her first lessons in music from Georg Benda, musical director at the court of Gotha, and her first ballet lessons under a Frenchman named Mereau. She was soon appearing regularly in children's roles. When the family returned to Breslau, where a Herr Weininger was the ballet master, her dance training was intensified and she had her first taste of personal success in the Italian pantomimes so popular during the eighteenth century.

Henriette was ten when the family moved again, this time to Berlin. Although everyone thought that the child was destined to be a dancer, she began to study declamation and mime under the renowned Professor J. J. Engel, who was then working on the book which was to make him famous. This was his *Ideen zu einer Mimik (Ideas on Mime)*, which appeared in Berlin in 1785, crystallizing his years of study of gesture and expression.

Although all of her short life had been spent in the theatre, Henriette made her "adult" debut at the age of thirteen, as leading ingenue in the private theatrical company maintained by Count Heinrich von Schwedt at his residence in Schwedt-on-the-Oder. Here Henriette acted, danced, and even sang the demanding coloratura role of Zerlina in Mozart's *Don Giovanni*.

Ever precocious, she married her first husband, the tenor Friedrich Eunicke, at sixteen. Together they appeared in Mainz, and it was here that, quite by accident, she discovered her extraordinary talent for mime. Cast in the role of a girl who loses her powers of speech at the sight of her murdered lover, and is obliged to communicate only by gesture, Henriette achieved a deeply moving characterization, which brought her a resounding success.

Just then, when Mainz was ready to acknowledge her genius, the French Revolution broke out and the young couple fled first to Bonn, then to Amsterdam, and finally, in 1794, back to Frankfurt, Germany. Here, in the studio of the painter Pforr, the impressionable young actress first saw Frederick Rehberg's drawings of Lady Hamilton's "attitudes."

For her own amusement and the entertainment of her husband's guests, Emma Hamilton, muse of Lord Nelson, favorite model of Romney, and one of the celebrated beauties of her day, had devised a series of expressive poses based on Greek sculpture. In Sir William Hamilton's drawing room at Naples, Goethe witnessed her performance and described it in his diary, on March 16, 1787:

He (Hamilton) has had a Graecian robe made for her which becomes her extremely well. She puts it on, lets her hair down, drapes a pair of shawls around her and then assumes such a variety of attitudes, postures and expressions that you think you must be dreaming . . . One moment she is standing, then she is seated, then reclining, then kneeling at your feet. Now she is solemn. Now she is sad. Now she is teasing, now enticing, bashful, alluring, reproachful or shy . . . One follows upon the other and the one emerges out of the other. She drapes her shawls to suit her every pose and changes them about to enhance it. She can make a hundred kinds of headdress out of those two shawls . . .

Frederick Rehberg, a painter attached to the German embassy at Rome, sketched Emma Hamilton in her "attitudes" and, in 1794, published a volume of engravings based upon these studies. It was this book which first inspired the eighteen-year-old Henriette Eunicke to create her own series of "living pictures," but where Lady Hamilton's attitudes were merely a parlor amusement, the German dancer and actress was to develop her studies into a full-length professional evening's entertainment with which she toured Germany, Scandinavia and even Russia for more than a decade. She might even be said to have given the first concerts of modern expressionistic dance.

In spite of her dreams of creative and individual expression, Henriette had a thoroughly professional attitude towards the theatre, and she was to undergo a long apprenticeship before she attempted to appear as a solo performer. In 1796 she went to Berlin, where she was soon accepted as a member of the national theatre. Her first marriage was dissolved in 1797, and she next married a physician, Dr. Meyer. It was under his name, as Henriette Meyer, that she played such roles as Phaedra, Medea, and Joan of Arc, gradually attaining recognition as Berlin's leading tragic actress.

Tragedy in her personal life brought this phase of her career to an abrupt close. Her husband, Dr. Meyer, fell in love with another woman. She agreed to a divorce, but, half-crazed with grief at the separation, she fled from Berlin, breaking her contract and abandoning the stage.

Like Isadora a century later, Henriette had a passionate love of children, and, as in the case of Isadora, motherhood was to bring her overwhelming sorrow. In her lifetime she bore sixteen children, yet she outlived thirteen of them, and four of her sons committed suicide.

At this time, however, she had two children who were being cared for in a pension in Stettin. She joined them there. A little later, in 1806, she married her third husband, another physician, Dr. Hendel, in Stettin. This was her happiest but shortest marriage, for just seven months later he died of typhus.

Desperate at her loss, and seeking for something to help her forget, she decided to return to the stage. However, the powerful director of the Berlin theatre, Iffland, had not forgotten her previous sudden defection, and refused to engage her again. Completely broken, she sought refuge in the home of her father-in-law, in the small town of Halle. She certainly did not dream that her greatest success was in the future.

In Halle, she met her fourth and last husband, a professor of philosophy, Dr. R. J. Schütz. This man was to help her achieve European renown, and to bring her a personal unhappiness more bitter than any she had previously experienced.

Through her entire career, Henriette had never ceased to study dancing and mime, and to experiment with her own plastic dances, based on mythology and ancient sculpture. Now Professor Schütz encouraged her to undertake a serious study of archaeology. She went to Dresden to work under the distinguished archaeologist, Dr. Boettiger, and was profoundly influenced by the masterpieces of early German and Italian renaissance painting found there. Her experimental dances and plastic pictures took on a more definitive form. She was now thirty-six, at the height of her beauty, rich in experience, and ready to perform as a creative artist.

It was a trick of fate, however, that actually launched her on her new career. The Napoleonic wars were raging; the little Corsican dictator, in his eastward march, closed the University of Halle and left Dr. Schütz without an occupation. Burningly ambitious, both for himself and his wife, he threw all his energies into assisting in her performances and organizing her tours. He did this so efficiently that, after her first solo performance in November 1808, she appeared with unparalleled success all over Germany, Denmark, Sweden, Holland, Russia and (after peace was restored and Napoleon banished from the scene) even in France.

What were her performances actually like? Anyone who has seen the Madonnas of Angna Enters, and those dances of Ruth St. Denis inspired by Egypt and Greece, should have little difficulty in picturing Henriette Hendel-Schütz's "plastic images." The performance began with an introductory lecture by Dr. Schütz, in which he briefly sketched the history of dance-pantomime from Greek and Roman times to the more recent work of Noverre and Angiolini. He then explained that it was his wife's ambition to restore the place of mime as one of the fine arts, and that she had attempted to develop it to such a degree of perfection that speech was unnecessary to the expression of a dramatic or pictorial theme.

Henriette used a small stage, with a severely plain black or gray backcloth, which one critic compared to a virgin canvas on which she painted an infinite variety of pictures. She never used a front curtain, but walked on stage and took her first position in full view of the audience.

Unlike Lady Hamilton, she sometimes used musical accompaniment, although for certain themes she moved in silence. At times she changed very slowly from one pose to another (as Enters does in her Madonnas); in others she achieved a frenzy which a critic called *bacchantisch*. If her pictures are to be believed, she worked barefoot, and was perhaps the first dancer to do so in recent history; even Lady Hamilton always wore ballet slippers or sandals. Usually she danced alone, but in some of her tableaux, including her favorite, *Niobe*, she was assisted by one or more of her children.

Her choice of themes was eclectic. Her program usually began with two Egyptian figures, first Isis, then the Sphinx. Next she turned to ancient Greece, with a Caryatid, then Galatea as she awoke under the touch of Pygmalion, then a tragic Niobe. Other subjects were a dying Magdalene, Cassandra, Agrippina, Ariadne, Hagar in the desert, an early German Madonna, and a whole scene from Shakespeare's *Tempest*, that in which Miranda first sees Fernando.

Hendel was deeply influenced by the ballets of Vincenzo Galeotti, which she saw in Copenhagen. Through his work she learned to apply the theories of Angiolini and Noverre to her own art, although after childhood she never worked in the medium of the classic ballet. As an old woman, she used to sit at the piano playing the score of Galeotti's ballet *Romeo and Juliette*, and explaining the dramatic situations to a friend. Suddenly she would jump up from the piano and mime an entire scene with tremendous clarity and power.

She was amazingly progressive in her use of costume. During her early days as an actress in Berlin, she had startled her colleagues by wearing a simple Greek tunic (instead of a paniered skirt) when she played Medea, and having her dresses copied from drawings by Albrecht Dürer and Lucas Cranach when she acted German roles. She preferred heavy woolen materials which would fall into decorative folds, and was a forerunner of Ruth St. Denis in her effective use of drapery. A past mistress of make-up and characterization, she had been able to impersonate old women convincingly while still in her 'teens, and now, as she approached middle age, brought a deceptive freshness and grace to her portraits of young women.

Illumination by gas had not yet been invented, to say nothing of electricity, when Henriette began her experiements with stage lighting. She hated the rows of candles at the front of the stage which served as footlights, so she devised a machine which would hold eighty wax candles, and which, placed in the wings, out of sight of the audience, would illuminate one side of the stage only, casting interesting shadows on the other.

While travelling from Finland to Sweden by boat, in 1812, Henriette met the famous Madame de Staël. A severe storm caused the captain of the little ship to seek temporary refuge in the harbor of a small island in the Baltic Sea. Here Henriette diverted her stranded fellow-passengers with an improvised performance, and later Madame de Staël wrote that "one person, through the power of her imagination, made me see the pictures and statues of glorious Rome in the midst of the ice of the North."

Carl von Holtei declared that "her Madonnas were worthy of Rafael," Schiller dedicated a poem to her, Wilhelm Grimm of the beloved *Grimm's Fairy Tales* composed a whimsical fairy tale in verse for her, and Goethe wrote in her album:

To the dear, incomparable, feminine Proteus Henriette Hendel-Schütz with thanks for very beautiful, only too short hours.

Until the end of her life Henriette continued to use the name of her favorite husband, Dr. Hendel, although she often combined it with that of Professor Schütz. In 1809 the ambitious professor had arranged for the publication of a large volume of engravings of his wife, by Joseph Nicolaus Peroux, in Frankfurt. In 1815 he published an extensive collection of tributes to her by distinguished poets, critics and artists. Nevertheless, the frustration of his own career made him increasingly resentful and jealous of her success, and he finally became openly and unbearably hostile. He was an opportunist, and a mercenary one; Henriette was idealistic and sincere in her dedication to art. She was relieved when the University of Halle reopened, in 1818, and he was able to resume his professorial duties. She continued her independent career for two more years, terminating it with a guest engagement in Leipzig, in 1820. Ten years later she finally divorced Dr. Schütz. She was to make one final theatrical appearance in 1836, at the ducal court of Stargard, in Pommerania, where she was living at that time.

Already forgotten, the great actress and mime was sharply recalled to mind by a startling painting exhibited soon after this brief return to the stage. It showed her seated, in a simple dress, while in the background the veil of Mary Stuart, the helmet of Joan of Arc, the crown of Queen Isabella and other accessories of her theatrical career were shown covered with a huge, dusty spider web.

Strangely enough, Henriette's hopes for the future had been concentrated, not in any of her own sixteen children, but in her stepdaughter Thekla Schütz, the professor's daughter by an earlier marriage. Especially promising as a dancer, Thekla had studied under Galeotti while Henriette was performing in Copenhagen, and the noted ballet master of the Royal Theatre had offered to train her for nothing. Unfortunately this was impossible; Henriette needed her, for it was Thekla who appeared as Ismael in her study of Hagar, and as the last dying child in *Niobe*. Henriette seemed destined for tragedy in every personal relationship, for this talented girl died of scarlet fever before she was twenty.

In her retirement, Henriette turned to teaching. Again anticipating Isadora, she dressed her pupils in Greek tunics. She taught them speech, singing and declamation as well as dancing, and rehearsed with them endlessly, trying without success to transmit one spark of her own genius, so that her ideas might live. She died at seventy-seven, on March 4, 1849, in the little town of Coslin, where during her last years she made her home with a married daughter, Sappho Bensemann. A troupe of wandering actors—like those she had known in her childhood—escorted her to her grave, singing an elegy from *Romeo and Juliette*.

—*Dance Magazine*, June 1956

Alexandre Placide. (Harvard Theatre Collection)

IV: When Ballet Came to Charleston

AS ONE of the cultural centres of the Colonies, Charleston, on the coast of South Carolina, enjoyed theatrical performances long before American independence was won. The first professional dancer to appear in America was probably Henry Holt, who arrived in Charleston in the autumn of 1734, and opened a dancing school. He claimed to have "served his time under Mr. Essex jun. the most celebrated Master in England, and danced a considerable time at both Play-Houses."

Holt was undoubtedly instrumental in arranging what seems to have been the first ballet presented in America. Given with Otway's play *The Orphan*, on February 4, 1735, this was the "New Pantomimic Entertainment in Grotesque Characters, called, the *Adventures of Harlequin and Scaramouch, with the Burgo'master trick'd.*" Since Charleston did not yet have a theatre, the performance took place in the Courtroom, on the second floor of the Exchange building, overlooking the harbour. Holt, an enterprising fellow, seems to have been one of the prime instigators in the erection of the famous Dock St. Theatre, one of America's earliest playhouses, which was reconstructed in 1936, two centuries after its inauguration, and is in use today.

In 1765 one Thomas Pike advertised the first course in dance notation to be offered in the Colonies. In a quaint announcement in the *South-Carolina Gazette*, he declared that: —

Ladies and Gentlemen may be instructed very expeditiously on moderate terms in ORCHESOGRAPHY, (or the art of dancing by characters and demonstrative figures, wherein the whole art is explained with complete tables of all the steps used in dancing), the utility of which is very well known in Europe, as they are thereby enabled to detect all pretenders to that science.

The wording of the notice leads one to believe that Pike's text was John Weaver's translation of Feuillet.

Dancing masters thrived in the prosperous southern port, but Charleston was not to enjoy full-scale ballet performances until 1794. By that time the country was independent and the theatre, under a ban during the Revolution, had been restored to favour.

The French revolution and the race riots in Santo Domingo sent large numbers of refugees to the United States. In the spring of 1794 a small band of gifted and experienced French theatrical artists—singers, dancers, actors, painters and musicians—arrived in Charleston. Among them were two men adept at choreography and production, and their combined efforts gave Charleston its first resident ballet company, and several seasons of ballet performances of great quality and range.

The guiding spirit of the French troupe was Alexandre Placide, a versatile actor, rope-dancer, acrobat, mime, and entrepreneur, who for several seasons had been appearing in New York, Boston, and Philadelphia. His background included a season or two in the Paris Opéra ballet school, a long apprenticeship under Nicolet at the popular Paris theatre known (by Royal permission) as *Les Grands Danseurs du Roi*, appearances at Sadler's Wells, and finally a sojourn in the West Indies. There he had acquired as "wife" (later events were to prove that they were never legally married) an attractive, accomplished, and very young French ballerina, Suzanne Vaillande, who was to win fame and notoriety in the United States under the name of "Madame Placide."

The principal classical dancer and choreographer was Jean Baptiste Francisqui, born in Bordeaux, probably of Basque descent. His early years are obscure, but he probably studied under Maximilien Gardel, and danced in Marseilles. On his arrival in the United States, he had a fairly thorough knowledge of the ballet repertoire of the chief French theatres. Credit for choreography was seldom given in American playbills of the day, but Francisqui was apparently responsible for the Charleston productions of such famous ballets as *The Whims of Galatea* (Noverre's *Caprices de Galathée*), *La Chercheuse d'Esprit* (originally by Maximilien Gardel, and the favourite vehicle of Marie Madeleine Guimard) and *Mirza and Lindor* (a "Grand, historical, tragi-heroic Pantomime in 3 acts," probably based on Gardel's *Mirza*).

In 1793 a new and elegant theatre had been erected in Charleston, but since this was leased by a company of American actors, the French newcomers were obliged to appear in a smaller playhouse, on Church Street. Here the French Theatre opened on April 10, 1794, with a programme including Jean Jacques Rousseau's musical interlude, *Pygmalion*, and a "grand ballet pantomime," *The Three Philosophers, or the Dutch Coffee House*. Dance roles were filled by Francisqui, M. and Mme.

Val, and M. Dainville, a singer who often filled in as a mime. Placide and a colleague named Spinacuta (another alumnus of Sadler's Wells) danced on the tight rope.

On the following evening, Mme. Placide made her début as Rosetta in another "grand ballet pantomime," *The Bird Catchers*. This popular little work, which Placide had introduced in New York two years earlier, was a mainstay of American ballet repertoire during the late eighteenth century. It probably derived from *Les Oiseleurs*, staged by Antoine Pitrot in Paris in 1759.

April 21, 1794, saw the production of the pantomime *Robinson Crusoe*, with Francisqui as Friday, and Master Louis Duport making his début in the *"Grande Folie d'Espagne*, with variations," which was interpolated in the second act. This Master Duport is an intriguing figure. He had arrived in the United States with his father, Pierre Landrin Duport, a dancer and composer, early in 1790. A child prodigy, young Duport appeared with extraordinary success as both violinist and dancer at concerts in Baltimore and Philadelphia. Eventually Pierre Landrin Duport opened a dancing school in the Federal Street Theatre, Boston. Louis, aged thirteen, turned up alone in Charleston, and for the next two years was one of the brightest stars of the ballet company. Too young to play romantic roles, he usually danced the most spectacular divertissements, and his name was prominently featured in the bills whenever he appeared. Among the ballets in which he danced were *Blaise et Babet, Jupiter and Europa, La Forêt Noire*, and *Le Déserteur Français*. He had particular success, with a solo, the *Chaconne de Punchinello*. In 1796, at fifteen, he disappeared from the American scene. Until the mystery of the parentage and early training of the great dancer Louis Antoine Duport is clarified, it is difficult to ignore the possibility that he and the "American" Louis Duport were identical.[1]

Another precocious child was Miss Duthé, who was ten when she made her début as a shepherdess in the ballet *The Rose and the Bud*, April 24, 1794. In the autumn the company was augmented by another refugee from Santo Domingo, Peter Fayolle, who made his first appearance on October 11 as Alexis in *The Whims of Galatea*.

By this time the French dancers had transferred to the more commodious Charleston Theatre, where Alexandre Placide was able to produce spectacular pantomimes. The newer theatre was well equipped with machinery for "transformations" and special effects, and there was a good orchestra. Scenery was painted by the skilled artists Audin and Belzon. Pantomimes now added to tne repertoire included *The Four Valiant Brothers*, popular in France as *Les Quatre Fils Aymon*, the topical

14th July, 1789, or, The Destruction of the Bastille, and *La Forêt Noire*, a melodramatic affair which starred Mme. Placide and a handsome opera singer named Louis Douvillier, who was versatile enough to play mime roles on occasion. In December, Francisqui produced *Le Déserteur Français*, "a grand Tragic Comic Ballet Pantomime, embellished with new dances, battles, military evolutions, etc., as presented with unbounded applause at the theatres in London, Paris, and all the principal cities in Europe." This was probably a version of Jean Dauberval's famous ballet *Le Déserteur*.

During the long season of 1794-95 dancing was featured, along with opera and drama, at almost every performance at the Charleston Theatre. Twenty-nine different ballets and pantomimes were produced, and some were repeated many times.

At the end of this prolific season, Jean Baptiste Francisqui left Charleston for engagements in the north. In 1796, nevertheless, Placide revived Francisqui's works and staged new ones, and the ballet shone nearly as brightly as before. Lovely Suzanne — still not quite eighteen — reigned as ballerina. Master Duport danced everything from classic solos to the Fandango and the Hornpipe. Francisqui's roles were taken over by Louis Douvillier. Tall and well built, with dark, wavy hair, he managed to carry off each part with a flair, although his forte was not ballet, but opera. His success with Suzanne Placide was somewhat greater than Alexandre had bargained for.

In the summer of 1796, Charleston was rocked by a scandal of major proportions. Placide challenged Douvillier to a duel, charging alienation of Suzanne's affections. Both men were skilled swordsmen — the playbills had often featured mock combats between them — but fortunately the affair terminated after Douvillier had received a surface wound, and Placide considered his honour avenged. A few days later, Douvillier married Suzanne — to the surprise of those who had known her as Mme. Placide — and they left Charleston. The dancer's later triumphs — and she enjoyed a long and brilliant career, as ballerina and, later, choreographer — were earned as Mme. Louis Douvillier.

Within a month Alexandre Placide got married, too. His choice was a seventeen-year-old English actress, Charlotte Wrighten. The shock of this marriage, so soon after the duel and its attendant scandal, actually killed Charlotte's mother, Mrs. Mary Ann Pownall, who died twelve days after the ceremony. On August 24, Charlotte's sister Mary died of grief. It was a tragedy on Shakespearean scale. Ironically enough, Charlotte and Alexandre Placide lived happily for many years, and raised five children who became such fine actors that for half a century they were the glory of the American stage.

The best days of the Charleston ballet were over, however. Although Charlotte Placide, under her husband's tuition, became a pleasing dancer, she remained primarily an actress. The Charleston ballet enjoyed another brief period of splendour in 1799, when Jean Marie Legé and his wife, from Paris via the West Indies, were engaged as leading dancers. Old ballets were revived and new ones produced—among them, an elaborate pantomime for February 22, called *The Birth Day of Genl. George Washington, or, The Triumph of Virtue.*

Ballet and pantomime held a prominent place in the Charleston repertoire until the death of Placide in 1812, but subsequent seasons did not attain the richness of those of the last decade of the eighteenth century. Today, Charleston is a one-night stop for touring ballet companies.

—*Dancing Times*, December 1956

[1] Lillian Moore explored this theory in greater detail in *The Duport Mystery (Dance Perspectives* No. 7). —I.G.

John Durang in the character of a Pas Seul à Vestris. (From the Collections of The Historical Society of York County, Pennsylvania)

V: New York's First Ballet Season, 1792

HE THEATRICAL DANCE played a relatively small part in the dramatic entertainments enjoyed in the American Colonies. Social dancing, of course, was popular everywhere; country dances and the more elegant minuet flourished even in puritanical New England. The various companies of actors who appeared from time to time in all the important cities of the Eastern seaboard usually included one or two performers agile enough to entertain between the acts with a Hornpipe or a comic dance. Pantomimes were occasionally produced, and the leading actors were skilled in the acrobatic antics required of Harlequin and Pantaloon.

Classic ballet, however, was represented only by a handful of individual artists who happened to visit the country from time to time. As early as 1738 Henry Holt, a dancer and teacher who had been trained in London by the celebrated Mr. Essex, presented "A New Pantomime Entertainment in Grotesque Characters, called The Adventures of Harlequin and Scaramouch, or, The Spaniard Trick'd," at the Long Room where he gave lessons.[1] The "Monsieur Denoier" who danced in Williamsburg in 1751 was undoubtedly a member of the well-known Desnoyers family, which furnished dancers to the principal theatres of Paris and London throughout the century. This particular "Denoier" gave a "Grand Tragic Dance . . . call'd the Royal Captive, after the *Turkish* Manner, as performed at His Majesty's Opera House in the Hay Market," after a performance of Shakespeare's *Richard III* at the New Theatre, Williamsburg, on October 21, 1751.[2] Pietro Sodi, a former star of the opera houses of Paris, Berlin, and Vienna, danced briefly in New York in 1774[3], but he was already an old man, more interested in earning a quiet living by teaching, than in performing. In 1783 a minor member of the Paris Opéra Ballet, Louis Roussel, danced Jack in *The Wapping Landlady, or, Jack in Distress,* a "Pantomimic Dance" produced by Dennis Ryan's company in New York.[4] This little work, popular in America until the close of the century, was probably closer to the form which we know as ballet than anything previously seen here.

It was not until after the French Revolution, however, that professional dancers came to the United States in any appreciable numbers. During the last decade of the eighteenth century America's budding culture was enriched by ballet performances of considerable variety and fairly impressive quality, organized chiefly by artists who had fled from the holocaust in France.

It was in 1792 that New York City enjoyed its first extended season of ballet and pantomime. The John Street Theatre was then under the management of Lewis Hallam and John Henry, leaders of the popular and well-established Old American company of actors, which had been playing in New York since the previous October. Their productions had included a pantomime or two, in addition to the usual plays and farces, and occasionally a Hornpipe danced between the acts, but dancing had played a comparatively small part in their entertainments.

On January 24, 1792, the New York *Daily Advertiser* carried the following announcement:

THEATRE

Hallam and Henry respectfully inform the Public, they have engaged for a few nights, Monsieur Placide, first rope dancer to the king of France, and his troop, lately arrived in America, who have been received with singular applause in the Theatres royal of Dublin, Bath, Bristol, and Norwich; also at Sadler's Wells. Monsieur Placide has sent for his performers from the southward, who may be expected in the course of ten or twelve days. The managers will give the earliest notice of their arrival, and flatter themselves, the united exertions in agility and pantomime, of these much applauded strangers, will prove acceptable to their generous friends and patrons.

The same paper, on the following day, announced the debut of M. and Mme. Placide, to take place that evening in the "dancing ballot" *The Bird Catcher.* Placide played the title role, his wife danced Rosetta, and the Hunters were Messrs. Durang, Martin, and Robinson, regular members of the Old American company who were already known as dancers, as well as actors. John Durang, as a matter of fact, was the first native American to become a professional dancer, while John E. Martin occasionally functioned as choreographer as well as performer.

Alexandre Placide, "first rope dancer to the king of France," was a colorful character whose swash-buckling escapades and amorous adventures had made him notorious from Dublin to Santo Domingo. He was a talented and versatile man of the theatre, celebrated as a tight-rope dancer (probably the very best of his time), acrobat, mime, actor, choreographer, and manager. Born in Paris in 1750,[5] he was the son of a pair of strolling players billed as "Signor and Signora Placido," although their family name was Bussa or Bussart. Alexandre's sister, Catherine-Ursule (known by her married name, Mme Billioni) had been one of the most brilliant actresses of the Comédie Italienne, before her death in 1783 at the age of thirty-two.[6]

Placide was a trained dancer, and may have been the man of that name who danced for a season (1771-72) in the ensemble of the Paris Opéra Ballet.[7] He won celebrity, however, as the star performer of the Théâtre de Nicolet on the Boulevard du Temple, the lively center of popular Paris entertainment. Largely through his sensational exploits on the tight-rope, which had attracted the attention of the king, Nicolet's troupe had earned the right to call itself Les Grands Danseurs du Roi.[8] Between his engagements in Paris, Placide had toured widely on the Continent and in the British Isles, usually with his inseparable companion Paulo Redigé, known as le Petit Diable, who was also his most formidable rival on the rope.

In 1781 Placide and the Little Devil (his name anglicized for the occasion) appeared at Sadler's Wells Theatre, London, where they added the art of English pantomime to their various accomplishments. Their mentor was old Giuseppe Grimaldi, whose three-year-old son Joey, making his precocious debut that same season, was to grow up to become the great comedian Joseph Grimaldi, "king of clowns."[9]

When Placide returned to Paris in the autumn, he produced several pantomimes he had learned in London. Still later, the same works appeared in the repertoires of the American theatres with which he was associated. One of Placide's colleagues of the Grands Danseurs du Roi, and heroine of his pantomime productions at about this time, was the lovely young Marie-Elisabeth Anne Roubert, known as Mlle. Miller. Later she became Mme. Pierre Gardel, the most distinguished ballerina of the Paris Opéra.[10]

In 1788 Placide left Europe for Santo Domingo, where he spent several adventurous and profitable seasons.[11] It was there, apparently, that he encountered Suzanne Vaillande, the very young and gifted dancer whom he brought to New York as his partner, "Madame Placide." Born in Dole, France, Suzanne was educated in Paris,[12] and may have been a pupil at the ballet school of the Paris Opéra. Her early years are obscure, however, and nothing definite is known about her life before she turned up in New York in 1792, already recognized as an unusually accomplished dancer, although she was not yet fourteen.

The Bird Catcher, the ballet in which the Placides made their American debut, was probably not an original composition of Placide's. It may have been based on Carlo Goldoni's *Gli Uccellatori,* a comic opera with music by Florian Leopold Gassman, which had been produced in Venice early in 1759.[13] A ballet called *Les Oiseleurs,* staged by Antoine Louis Bonaventure Pitrot, was given at the Comédie Italienne, Paris, later that same year.[14] In 1792 *Gli Uccellatori* was presented as a ballet in Bologna, with choreography by Carlo Fiorillo,[15] while in that same year Antonio Muzzarelli staged the ballet *Der Vogelsteller,* with music by Franz Xaver Süssmayer, in Vienna.[16] Although Placide's *Bird Catcher* was singular, it became *The Bird Catchers* in later productions when the choreographer had a larger company of dancers to draw upon. Probably the simplification was a matter of expediency, since the other members of Placide's troupe had not yet arrived "from the southward," and the burden of the performance was borne by the two Placides themselves. In addition to appearing in *The Bird Catcher,* they danced the *Minuet de la Cour* and a *Gavotte,* while the Old American company presented *The Suspicious Husband* and a farce, *Seeing is Believing.*

By February 3 the rest of Placide's associates, including his old friend and colleague the Little Devil, had arrived in New York. They made their bow in another "dancing ballet" (Placide, in his advertisements, was careful to make the nature of the entertainment quite clear) called *The Two Philosophers, or, The Merry Girl,* "in which Madame Placide will dance a HORNPIPE." It was further announced that Placide (who, at the age of forty-two, had lost none of his youthful agility — he was to continue to dance on the rope until he was fifty-eight) would "somerset backward and forward, over a table and a chair," and "dance a Hornpipe on the rope, jump over a cane, play the fiddle in different ways, &c." in addition to appearing in the ballet.[17] *The Two Philosophers* became quite a favorite, and was to reappear frequently in the Placide repertoire during his subsequent engagements in other American cities.

February 6 saw the première of the first pantomime staged by Placide in New York. This was *Harlequin Protected by Cupid, or, The Enchanted Nosegay,* given with Shakespeare's *King Henry the Fourth.*[18] Throughout this season, the bills at the John St. Theatre usually consisted of a play, a ballet or pantomime, interludes of dancing or acrobatics, and perhaps a farce for good measure.

Another "dancing ballet," *The Return of the Labourers,* was given for Alexandre Placide's benefit on February 8.[19] This featured a *Sabottière Dance,* in which the rhythmic click-clack of wooden shoes gave the New Yorkers an early taste of something like the tap dancing which has since become so universally popular, and is considered so typically American!

The ballet *The Wood Cutters*, with an *Allemande* by M. and Mme. Placide, was presented on February 10 (*Adv* Feb 10). This was certainly *Les Bucherons* (sometimes called *Les Bucherons amoureux et rivaux*), a ballet produced by Nicolet's *Grands Danseurs du Roi* in Paris on November 5, 1785,[20] when Placide was in the company. This in turn may have derived from the pantomime *The Wood Cutters*, in which Placide, the Little Devil, and Giuseppe Grimaldi had appeared at Sadler's Wells, London, on September 16, 1781.[21]

Very few playbills of this first New York dance season have survived, and it is only occasionally possible to establish the casting of a ballet or pantomime. In *The Restoration of Harlequin*, which had its first performance February 13, Placide was Pierrot, the Little Devil was the Old Man, the American dancer John Martin was the Lover, the actor Stephen Woolls was the Sorcerer, and Mme. Placide was Columbine (Odell I 303). Harlequin was danced by Simonet, a member of Placide's company who remains a mysterious figure although he bore a famous name. A François Simonet had danced under the direction of the celebrated choreographer Jean Georges Noverre in Vienna[22] and London, and was for several seasons ballet master at the King's Theatre, London.[23] Adelaide Simonet was Noverre's prima ballerina at the Haymarket Theatre, London, in 1781.[24] Other members of the Simonet family danced in Paris and Stockholm in the 1790s. The exact identity of the man who appeared with Placide in 1792, and his possible relationship to François Simonet, has not been established.

The career of Paulo Redigé, the Little Devil, is easier to trace. He was the son of Jean Redigé, who ran a small theatre on the Boulevard du Temple. Both Paulo and his sister, known as *la Petite Saxonne*, were trained as dancers and acrobats from childhood.[25] As *le Petit Diable*, the name he used for the rest of his career, Redigé made his debut at the Foire Saint-Germain in 1779, and sprang into immediate popularity. Little more than a child, he had extraordinary daring, and performed seemingly impossible feats. One of his tricks was dancing on the tight-rope with eggs tied to his feet, without breaking one.[26]

Placide and the Little Devil had great success with their famous *Danse du Drapeau*, in which they displayed flags in various decorative positions while dancing on the rope. In London, at a time of high political tension between England and France, they were attacked by a furious mob when they dared to display the fleur-de-lys in this exhibition. They barely escaped with their lives. When they got back to France, however, they took great pains to flaunt their independence of any particular patriotism by appearing everywhere wearing typical English clothing, and mounted on English horses.[27] Placide often performed his Flag Dance in New York, but presumably he used the brand-new Stars and Stripes instead of the arms of France. At any rate, the number never provoked any controversy.

Unlike Placide, who was to spend the rest of his life in the United States, Redigé returned to Europe after a comparatively short time. He married a Spanish rope dancer, Mlle Malaga, known as *la belle Espagnole*. Their son, billed simply as Paulo, was a contemporary and rival of Joseph Grimaldi on the London stage, and descendants of this family were still active in the London theatre as late as 1925.[28]

The "historic pantomime" *The Old Soldier* was Placide's next production, on February 15 (*Adv* Feb 15). Taken from a French original, *Le Maréchal des Logis, ou le Bon Coeur d'un Soldat Français,* this is one of the few dance works seen in New York during the eighteenth century for which a libretto of sorts has survived. When Placide produced it in Charleston, a few years later, he published the following note about it: "This Pantomime is taken from a true STORY which happened within ten years in a Forest four leagues from Paris. An old Veteran who is dismissed from his regiment, on his way to Paris delivers a Young Girl from the hands of two thieves, whom he kills, and restores her to her friends."[29]

The first New York performance advertised a "fight with Sabres, between the Old Soldier and the Two Thieves," but the cast was not announced. On the playbill for a later performance (April 24) it was listed as follows:

The Old Soldier	Monsieur Placide
Lucas	Mr. Martin
The Two Thieves	The Little Devil and Mons. Dumas
Clown	Mr. Durang
The Lord of the Manor	Mr. Harper
Milk Maid	Mrs. Gray
Collate [i.e., Collette]	Madame Placide[30]

This cast was a nice mixture of actors from the Old American company, and French dancers.

For Mme. Placide's benefit performance, two days later, a new three-act "heroic pantomime," *La Belle Dorothée,* was produced (*Adv* Feb 17). Some details of this work, which had been prominent in the repertoire of the Théâtre de l'Ambigu-Comique during Placide's Paris days, may be gleaned from the rather confused description in advertisements of his Charleston production of it two years later:

The first act passes in a camp near the city of Orleans at the time when the English besieged it. . . . [It] represents a combat at a distance and the reception of a Knight from the fashion of ancient times, with all the pomp that then existed, afterwards the departure of the troops and that of the French general to rejoin his dear Dorothée. The other three acts pass at Milan in Italy. . . . In the last act will be a procession used in Italy, called an Auto da Fé, where Dorothée is conducted to the pile to be burnt, as a victim to the jealousy of her uncle. A combat of swords and daggers between Sacrogargon and La Tremouille, when the former falls, and the courage of La Tremouille saves Dorothée from the middle of the flames.[31]

Although the Charleston version had four acts and the New York production only three, it may be assumed that they were substantially the same and that the talented beneficiary played the title role at this American première as she did later in Charleston. At a star's benefit, it was customary to include some special attraction, and on this occasion Suzanne Placide danced for the first time on the tight rope. She called attention to this extra feature in her advertisements: "Mrs. Placide presents her compliments to the Ladies and Gentlemen of this city, and hopes from the variety of the entertainment, and her exertions to please the public, that she will have the honor of their company" (Adv Feb 17). The feat of mastering the rope does not seem to have given her much artistic satisfaction, however, for she repeated it only a few times in her entire career.

Although no description of her performance as Dorothée has survived, we know from one of her contemporaries that Suzanne was "eminently beautiful,"[32] while William Dunlap considered her an "excellent dancer and pantomime actress."[33] Noah M. Ludlow, who saw her many years later, described her as "tall and commanding in her bearing, fine hair and eyes, splendid bust, and beautifully rounded figure," and declared, "I have never seen such truly *speaking* pantomime. . . ."[34]

A new "dancing ballet," *The Old Schoolmaster Grown Young,* was the next attraction, on February 20 (Adv Feb 20). This featured an *Allemande* by M. and Mme. Placide. The *Allemande,* a theatrical adaptation of a social dance popular in the ballrooms of the time, was characterized by the complicated turns and evolutions executed by partners turning under each others' arms, with their hands joined. George Balanchine, in some of his most intricate and advanced twentieth-century choreographic inventions, is often inspired by the same sort of interweaving of partners with clasped hands.

Columbine Invisible, or, Harlequin Junior, a pantomime which Placide had produced in Paris for the *Grands Danseurs du Roi,*[35] was given on

February 24, with new scenery, machinery, and decorations (*Adv* Feb
24). The cast included Placide as Pierrot, Mme. Placide as Columbine,
Martin as Harlequin Junior, Mr. Robinson as Harlequin Senior, Mrs.
Rankin as Harlequin's Mother, the Little Devil as the Old Man, Mr.
Hammond as the Lover, and Monsieur Dumas as the Constable (Odell I
303). Again the French and American performers had combined their
forces.

The feature of Alexandre Placide's gala benefit, February 29, was *The
Indian Heroine, or, Inkle and Yarico,*[36] a pantomime version of Samuel
Arnold's opera *Inkle and Yarico,* first given in London in 1787. The opera
had already been heard in New York in 1789,[37] but this 1792 performance seems to have marked the American première of the dance pantomime, which was frequently repeated all over the United States, sometimes under the title of *The American Heroine,* during the next quarter of
a century.

There were no new dance productions in the next few weeks, but *The
Bird Catcher, The Wood Cutters,* and *The Two Philosophers* were
repeated. The Placides volunteered to dance *The Bird Catcher* at Joseph
Harper's benefit performance on March 9, and he seems to have been
genuinely appreciative of their generosity, if one may judge from the note
which he inserted in the *Daily Advertiser* four days later:

Mr. HARPER acknowledges with the deepest gratitude, the many attentions he
has experienced from the friends of the drama, and his friends in particular, begs
leave to return them his sincere thanks for their kind patronage, at the play lately
performed for his benefit. To Mr. and Madame PLACIDE, he is under particular
obligations—their generous conduct in offering, and actually giving their
assistance to him, without any compensation, impresses him with every sentiment in their favour, and inspires the most hearty wishes for their prosperity.

John Martin, for his benefit on March 26, staged a new pantomime
called *The Silver Rock, or, Love and Magic.* Martin, then about twenty-
four years old, has been considered the first native American to become a
professional actor, as John Durang was the first American dancer. Their
careers overlapped. Martin, although he probably had little formal training, often appeared as a dancer, and the nimble Harlequin was one of his
favorite roles. (He played it now, in *The Silver Rock.*) At this performance
Placide and the Little Devil were advertised to "perform the Manual
Exercise on the Rope and display a Flag in various Attitudes," after the
play, but they did not participate in the pantomime which followed.
Martin drew his entire cast from the regular members of the Old American

company, with Miss Tuke, a charming actress but no dancer, as Columbine. The most spectacular feature of the production was "a grand Display of the Temple of Hymen, in transparency, with Harlequin and Columbine, attended by Cupid."[38]

A revival of a pantomime called *The King of the Genii, or, Harlequin Neptune,* which had been in the repertoire of the acting company before the arrival of the Placides, was announced for Mrs. Gray's benefit on April 16, but seems to have been postponed until two days later. Again John Martin played Harlequin to Miss Tuke's Columbine.[39]

The next new pantomime, *The Birth of Harlequin, or, The Witches' Frolic,* was given for the benefit of John Durang and Mr. Ashton on April 27. It was announced as "A new Comic pantomimical entertainment, never performed here, as performed at Sadler's Wells and at Philadelphia, with universal applause . . ." and it included a "Witches Broom-Dance" and a "Masquerade dance, in Grotesque characters" (*Adv* Apr 27).

Mme. Placide played Columbine to John Durang's Harlequin, which must have been a signal honor for the American dancer (Odell I 306). This piece had been given in Philadelphia for Durang's benefit on July 7, 1791,[40] and no doubt it was he who staged it on both occasions. In his Diary, preserved at the Historical Society of York, Pennsylvania, Durang called this "a good benefit. . . . at least I cleared $300 which was a great sum at the time."

Born in Lancaster, Pennsylvania, in 1768 (he was the same age as John E. Martin), John Durang had studied dancing under Louis Roussel and was already an experienced dancer and choreographer, although he could not be compared to the Placides in professional polish. He admired the French dancers greatly, and no doubt learned a great deal about ballet technique, stagecraft, and showmanship from them. Durang's career lasted well into the nineteenth century, and several of his children, including Charles Durang, historian of the Philadelphia theatre, became successful dancers.

For the joint benefit of M. and Mme. Placide, on May 3, there was another new pantomime called *Harlequin Balloonist, or, Pierrot in the Clouds.*[41] The balloon was a comparatively new invention, the first successful flight having taken place in France only ten years earlier, while it was not until eight months after Placide's production, in January 1793, that Pierre Blanchard was to make the first ascension in the United States. In *Harlequin Balloonist* Mme Placide danced a Hornpipe, as well as the *Minuet de la Cour* and an *Allemande.* Although the scenery was advertised as new, it would not be surprising to find that the "grand view of the

TEMPLE OF CUPID" was identical with the "Grand display of the TEMPLE OF HYMEN" which had graced *The Silver Rock* five weeks earlier.

Harlequin Balloonist was the last new dance production. The season closed on May 14 with an original farce by Mr. Robinson, a member of the company, called *The Yorker's Wedding, or, Banana's Stratagem,* a play, *The New Peerage,* an epilogue spoken by John Martin "in the character of a DRUNKEN SAILOR," rope dancing by Placide, Simonet, and the Little Devil, and a repeat performance of the ballet *The Two Philosophers, or, The Merry Girl,* with Mme. Placide dancing a Hornpipe (Adv May 14).

Because of the scarcity of dependable records, it is impossible to compile an absolutely complete and accurate list of all the performances which actually took place during New York's first ballet season. Sometimes scheduled performances were cancelled without notice, because of bad weather or the indisposition of an important player. As nearly as we have been able to estimate, however, twenty-seven performances of ballets and pantomimes were given (with various plays and farces) at the John St. Theatre between January 25 and May 14, 1792. These included five one-act ballets, all staged by Alexandre Placide; and ten pantomimes, ranging from one to three acts, of which one was a revival, one was produced by John Martin, and one by John Durang; Placide was responsible for the remaining seven. The most popular ballet was *The Two Philosophers,* given five times (unless the performances advertised for May 10 and 12 were postponed until May 14). *The Old Soldier* and *The Bird Catcher* were presented three times each, but several of the pantomimes were seen only once. (See Appendix.)

When the New York season closed, the Placides went with the American actors to Philadelphia for a summer engagement (Pollock 188– 190). In August, the dancers inaugurated the New Exhibition Room (a theatre in all but name) in Boston, where theatrical performances were still officially banned following the stringent laws adopted at the time of the Revolution.[42]

Early in 1794 the Placides settled in Charleston, where Alexandre was to spend the rest of his life. For many years he was the manager of the Charleston Theatre, producing original American plays and standard dramatic repertoire as well as the ballets and pantomimes with which he was originally associated.[43]

In 1796, Suzanne precipitated a major scandal in the Charleston theatre when her love affair with the handsome and gifted singer Louis Douvillier caused Placide to challenge him to a duel.[44] Douvillier was slightly wounded, and Suzanne promptly left Placide (to whom she had

never been legally married) to become his wife. About 1799 the Douvil-
liers went to New Orleans, where Suzanne enjoyed a long career as first
dancer and, later, America's first woman choreographer. She retired in
1818, and died in New Orleans on August 30, 1826.[45]

The Little Devil left the United States soon after the New York and
Philadelphia seasons of 1792. The later lives of Simonet and Dumas
remain a mystery. John Martin's brief career was devoted primarily to
acting, although he often danced in ballets and pantomimes, and occasionally staged them. He died on April 18, 1807, at the age of thirty-
nine.[46]

John Durang profited from the lessons he had learned from the
Placides. The story of his long and active career as America's first native-
born professional dancer has already been told in considerable detail.[47]

The Placides and their colleagues were popular and versatile enter-
tainers. They made no elaborate pretensions and their little ballets,
pantomimes, and acrobatic stunts were designed simply to please and to
amuse. Nevertheless Suzanne and Alexandre Placide were accomplished artists in their own way. Their first New York season heralded
a decade in which the ballet flourished in all the theatrical centers of the
United States. The Placides themselves, in Charleston, participated in
productions of ballets by Jean Georges Noverre and Maximilien Gardel,
staged by the prolific choreographer Jean Baptiste Francisquy. Before
she was murdered by her husband in 1798, the beautiful and mysterious
Anna Gardie starred in ballet-pantomimes in Philadelphia, New York,
and Boston. James Byrne, distinguished choreographer of London's
Covent Garden Theatre, brought such spectacular ballets as *Oscar and
Malvina, The Death of Captain Cook,* and *Dermot and Kathleen* to
Philadelphia in 1796. The Placides, with their first New York season,
were simply the avant-garde of America's first golden age of ballet.

At the beginning of the nineteenth century its brilliance faded somewhat, largely because the early performers had retired or returned to
Europe without training adequate successors. The climax of a second
resplendent period, when ballet was one of the most charming and
typical manifestations of the age of romanticism, came in 1840, when the
great Viennese ballerina Fanny Elssler visited the United States. Later,
over-emphasis on vulgar technical tricks caused another temporary
eclipse of the art.

Today, the wide-spread popularity of ballet in America rests on a solid
foundation. No longer is a ballet season the rare and exotic event it must
have seemed in 1792. Across the country, some of the finest ballet
schools in the world have trained magnificent American dancers, who fill

the ranks of companies with headquarters in New York, Chicago, San Francisco. These ballet companies not only delight audiences in the United States, but serve as cultural ambassadors in taking American art to the far corners of the world.

APPENDIX

Ballets and Pantomimes produced at the John St. Theatre. New York. by Alexandre Placide and his company of French dancers, with members of the Old American company of actors, January 25—May 14, 1792.

1 *La Belle Dorothée* / Heroic Pantomime, in 3 acts, Feb 17
2 *The Bird Catcher* / Ballet, Jan 25, Mar 9, Apr 9
3 *The Birth of Harlequin* / Pantomime, Apr 27
4 *Columbine Invisible, or, Harlequin Junior* / Pantomime, Feb 24
5 *Harlequin Balloonist, or, Pierrot in the Clouds* / Pantomime, May 3
6 *Harlequin Protected by Cupid, or, The Enchanted Nosegay* / Pantomime, Feb 6
7 *The Indian Heroine, or, Inkle and Yarico* / Historic Pantomime, in 3 acts, Feb 29
8 *The King of the Genii, or, Harlequin Neptune* / Pantomime, Apr 16, Apr 18 (This work had been in the repertoire before the arrival of the Placide company.)
9 *The Old Schoolmaster Grown Young* / Ballet, Feb 20, Apr 13
10 *The Old Soldier* / Historic Pantomime, with dancing, Feb 15, Feb 27, Apr 24
11 *The Restoration of Harlequin* / Pantomime, Feb 13
12 *The Return of the Labourers* / Ballet, Feb 8, Apr 30
13 *The Silver Rock, or, Love and Magic* / Pantomime, Mar 26 (The French dancers did not participate.)
14 *The Two Philosophers, or, The Merry Girl* / Ballet, Feb 3, Mar 23, May 10, May 12, May 14
15 *The Wood Cutters* / Ballet, Feb 10, Mar 12

For assistance in the research for this article I am very much indebted to Miss Genevieve Oswald, Curator of the Dance Collection, and to the staffs of the Music Division, the Rare Book Division, and the Theatre Collection of The New York Public Library; Dr. William Van Lennep and Miss Mary Reardon of the Harvard Theatre Collection; Mr. Patrick Carroll of the Walter Hampden Memorial Library, The Players, New York; Miss Virginia Rugheimer and the staff of the Charleston Library Society; Miss Margaret Moseman of the Charleston Free Library; Mme. Sylvie Chevalley, Joseph E. Marks III, Dr. Walter Toscanini, and Miss Alice M. Wyss.

—Bulletin of The New York Public Library, September 1960.

Footnotes to this article, *New York's First Ballet Season, 1792,* appear in the Appendix, page 155.

Alexander Reinagle. (Music Division, The New York Public Library)

VI: Ballet Music in George Washington's Time

BALLET was decidedly a lively art, in the America of George Washington. The most active theatrical centers of the original thirteen states were found in Philadelphia, Charleston, New York and (rather suprisingly when one considers its Puritan background and the fact that theatrical performances were forbidden there as late as 1792) in Boston. In those days, so long before television, films and radio were available to furnish light entertainment, a theatre was obliged to provide highly diversified fare in order to cater to the varied tastes of the people. As is still the case today in the smaller cities of Europe, it was customary for one theatre to present music, dance and drama, and examples of each category were usually to be found on each night's bill. Grand and comic opera, drama and farce, pantomime, brief dance interludes, and ballet in the grand manner were all familiar to the theatregoers of the time.

Ballet received a tremendous inpetus early in the 1790s, when the French Revolution and the uprisings in Santo Domingo sent a wave of refugee dancers to our shores. In Charleston during one season (1794-95), no less than twenty-nine different ballets and pantomimes were produced, in addition to the incidental dances given in almost every play and opera. To be sure, Charleston had the advantage, that season, of two gifted dancers who were also experienced choreographers: Francisquy, who seems to have served his apprenticeship in the ballet ensemble at the Paris Opéra, and Alexandre Placide, a versatile rope dancer, actor and mime who was adept at staging ballets and pantomimes from the repertoires of the various French and English theatres in which he had appeared.

When Francisquy moved on to Boston, in 1796, he made that city a center of ballet production. In Philadelphia, the same year, the engagement of the well-known English dancer and choreographer James Byrne, with his beautiful Italian wife, led to a brilliant period for ballet. In New

York the debut of a ballerina, the fascinating and mysterious Madame Gardie, brought new interest to the dance repertoire. In 1798, after four years on the American stage, this accomplished artist was murdered by her husband, under circumstances which have never been entirely clarified.

Most of the early American theatres had good sized permanent orchestras. That of the Federal Street Theatre, Boston, in 1796, consisted of seventeen men, including a violinist-conductor and a composer. The ensembles in Charleston and Philadelphia were probably considerably larger.

The selection of music for ballet in the eighteenth century was just as unsystematic as it is today. Light operas, such as those of Grétry, Monsigny and Duni, were a favorite source of ballet subjects, and the original music was often adapted for the dance version. (Roland Petit was merely following a custom a hundred and fifty years old, when he made a ballet of *Carmen*.) For example, *The Two Hunters and the Milkmaid*, a little comic ballet which was as much a staple of early American ballet repertoire as *Les Sylphides* and *Scheherazade* in this century, was an adaptation of Duni's *Les Deux Chasseurs et la Laitière*. Francisquy acknowledged his ballet *Blaise et Babet* to be a dance arrangement of Dezède's opera.

Then, as now, choreographers were fond of taking existing music and arranging their ballets without regard for the original meaning of the score. Lavalette's pantomine *The Princess of Babylon* given in Charleston in 1797, used music by Gluck (from *Iphigenie in Aulide*), Grétry (*Panurge dans l'Isle des Lanternes*) and Johann Christoph Vogel (*The Golden Fleece*). Francisquy used the overture to Paisiello's *Frescatana* in the score for his *The Unfortunate Family*. Then again, when he produced the "new grand tragic pantomime," *The New French Deserter,* Francisquy chose music by Grétry, although the opera *Le Déserteur* was by Monsigny, and Maximilien Gardel's ballet of the same title (which Francisquy claimed to be reproducing) had a score by Miller. It was not unusual for the name of the composer to be entirely omitted from the playbills and advertisements, especially when the ballet was well known and the music presumably familiar.

Sometimes the orchestra leader was a capable composer, as in the case of Alexander Reinagle in Philadelphia, and then the ballet master was lucky enough to have new scores tailored to measure. Reinagle wrote the music for the pantomimes *Harlequin's Invasion, Harlequin Shipwrecked*, and *The Witches of the Rock*; he compiled a score, using Irish and Scottish themes, for the "Grand Divertissement" in the Temple of Liberty, taken from the celebrated ballet, called *Warrior's Welcome Home*, and he provided a new overture for Madame Gardie's favorite vehicle, *La Forêt Noire*.

Members of the various theatre orchestras, and even the versatile and hard working singers and dancers were frequently pressed into service to compile ballet scores from popular sources, or to compose new ones. Benjamin Carr, Victor Pelissier, Louis Boullay and John Bentley were among the most active of these early performer-composers, and all of them wrote a great deal of dance music. When Jean Marie Legé staged a new ballet called *The Birthday or Rural Fete*, to be given in Boston in honor of Washington's birthday, on February 22, 1797, it had a score especially composed by Raynor Taylor, English-born pianist, organist and teacher, who had long been active in Baltimore and Philadelphia. On the other hand, when the ensemble dancer and violoncellist Renaud provided the score for Legé's Boston production of *The Island of Calypso, or the Adventures of Telemachus*, he may well have been setting down more or less what he remembered of Miller's score for the Paris version of the ballet, just as Legé undoubtedly based his choreography on the original version by Pierre Gardel.

For brief divertissements, dancers in early America were quick to capitalize on the popularity of catchy and familiar tunes, and it is not surprising to find that in 1797 Francisquy concluded one of his ballets, *The Cooper, or The Amorous Guardian*, with "a new Country Dance, called Yankee Doodle." Sometimes the fame of a particular dance ensured the widespread success of the music and it is only as the composer of *Durang's Hornpipe*, written for John Durang, the first native American to enjoy a career as a professional dancer, that the name of Franz Hoffmeister survives today.

In that practical age, ballet masters were their own accompanists. The violin, instead of the piano, was used at ballet rehearsals and classes, and every dancing teacher was of necessity a good violinist. His miniature violin, or "kit," was as indispensable an item of equipment as his ballet shoes. Sometimes dancers were also composers, and provided the music for their own ballets (as was the case with the Italian Gaspare Angiolini, Noverre's great rival in the development of dramatic ballet).

A prominent example of the dancer-composer in America was Pierre Landrin Duport, a refugee from the French Revolution, whose activities extended to Boston, New York, Philadelphia, Baltimore, Washington and points south. He preferred to work independently, as head of his own school, and was not regularly associated with the theatres in any of the cities where he taught. In Boston, however, he gave some fairly ambitious performances, with his pupils and guest stars. Legé danced in his *The Descent of Apollo* at the Haymarket Theatre in 1798. This had music by

Grétry. For another of his Boston productions, a ballet called *The May*, Duport composed his own music, and a fragment of it has survived in a collection of Duport manuscripts at the Library of Congress. The same collection includes a "fancy Menuit (sic) Dance before Genl Washington 1792" and a "fancy Menuit with figure Dance by two young Ladies in the presence of Mrs. Washington in 1792—Phila." Duport was a prolific composer of waltzes, cotillions and country dances, many of which were published during his lifetime. More recently, two of his minuets were chosen by Albert Stoessel for inclusion in his orchestral suite *Early Americana*, published in 1936.

—Etude, September 1956

Printed and published on Wednesdays and Saturdays, by BENJAMIN RUSSELL, Printer of the LAWs of the UNION, for the NORTHERN STATES—South side State-Street, next to the Coffee-House, BOSTON, (Massachusetts.)

SATURDAY, JULY 28, 1798.

[PRICE THREE DOLLARS, per ANNUM.]

Whole No. 1498.—No. 42, of VOL. XXIX.

Columbian ❀ Centinel

Three accounts of a melancholy event at *New-York*, July 20.

[FIRST.]

Yefterday morning, about 3 o'clock, Mr. GARDIE, went to his wife's bed, and, with a knife ftabbed her to the heart! Her fcreeches awoke her fon, about 10 years old —he got up, and, before he had time to leave the room, he faw Mr. GARDIE plunge the fame knife into his own belly! They both expired on the fpot! They were at lodgings at the noted French boarding-houfe, the corner of Pearl and Broad-ftreets. [*Thefe unfortunate perfons perfoimed feveral months on our Theatre.* CENT.]

[SECOND.]

Yefterday morning, between 3 and 4 o'clock, a moft dreadful circumftance occurred at a French boarding houfe, near the exchange in this city. Madame *Gardie*, late of the Theatre, was in bed with her fon about 11 years of age. Monfieur *Gardie*, who had cohabited with her a number of years, and who lodged in the fame room, got up, ordered the boy to rife, and got into the bed The boy hearing his mother cry out, afked what was the matter ?—Mr. *Gardie* defited him to lie ftill ; his mother had only fainted. Soon after, hearing a knocking againft the partition, he got up, and went to the bed, where he found Mr. *Gardie* in the agonies of death, and his mother lying dead in the bed.

It appears that he ftabbed her with a new carving knife, in the left breaft, which penetrated immediately to the heart, as fhe appears to have expired inftantly. He was wounded in the breaft in two places; with his own hand ; and muft have died in extreme agony, as he had fallen from the bed on the floor, and was covered with blood. The Coroner's Inqueft brought a verdict, that he was the caufe of her death, and afterwards committed fuicide,

The canfe of this very dreadful catraftophe, is attributed to extreme penury, and her refufing to accompany him to *France*, whether he was going fhortly, having taken his paffage. This refufal excited his jealoufy, altho there does not appear to be any grounds for the fufpicion.

[THIRD.]

Laft night a moft tragical circumftance took place in this city. Madam GARDIE and her hufband mutually agreed to, and actually did ftab each other, and are both dead ! They, it feems, were much reduced in pecuniary affairs, and fell upon this expedient to relieve themfelves ! Gracious God ! how wonderful are the effects of poverty on the minds of the proud.

Clipping from the *Columbian Centinel* for July 28, 1798, giving three accounts of Anna Gardie's murder. (Rare Book Division, The New York Public Library)

VII: The Slain Ballerina: Anna Gardie

"A BEAUTIFUL AND FASCINATING WOMAN . . . the charmer of all who approached her," was the way William Dunlap, first historian of the American theater, described Anna Gardie, the first real ballet star to perform in the United States. George Washington was President when she made her American debut. John Adams had just succeeded him when, four years later, she was murdered by a husband crazed with grief at the thought of parting from her.

Mme. Gardie excelled in roles which gave her extensive opportunities for emotional, melodramatic acting. *La Forêt Noire,* the ballet pantomime in which she made her bow at the New Theater, Philadelphia, on April 26, 1794, was a typical example. As a young mother desperately trying to save her kidnapped child from a band of Brigands, Anna Gardie was sensational. "The town were in ecstasies with her," wrote Charles Durang, "Truly beautiful . . . With splendid talents, she combined all the vivacious fascinations of her gay and polite nation."

New York, where she appeared later that same year, was just as enthusiastic. "Madame Gardie. . .gave us a delight altogether new," declared the *New York Magazine,* "Her face, figure and action were . . . prepossessing beyond any example on our stage."

Mystery shrouded much of the early life of the enchanting dancer. With her husband, a penniless young French nobleman, and her small son (by a previous union), she arrived in Philadelphia from Santo Domingo. She had appeared briefly on the stage there and in France. It was in the United States, however, that she won enduring fame.

There is a widespread belief that ballet was unknown in America until this century. (Pavlova, Nijinsky, and Sol Hurok are often mentioned among candidates for the honor of having introduced it!) Nevertheless, ballet was seen here two hundred years ago, and during the last decade of the eighteenth century it was a very popular form of entertainment.

French dancers were active in theatrical centers from Boston to New Orleans, and Mme. Gardie even numbered a few Americans among her ballet colleagues. John Durang (father of Charles) could cut an entrechat as well as dance a hornpipe!

An artist of enormous versatility, Mme. Gardie danced in ballets ranging from *The Sailor's Landlady* to Noverre's *Whims of Galatea.* She played Columbine in the Harlequinades, a Witch in *Macbeth,* America in *The Independence of America, or the Ever Memorable Fourth of July 1798.* A Boston paper declared that she had "a certain something in her action and expression, which ravishes the senses," while another marveled over her power "to melt, to fascinate, and astonish."

Then her fortunes changed. During the Revolution, France had been America's ally. Now political tensions between the two nations became so violent that every Frenchman was suspect. Ballet, considered a French art, lost its popularity. Managers were afraid to engage French dancers.

For a time Gardie managed to support his wife and her son by playing anonymously in theater orchestras. Then in the summer of 1798 the little family grew desperate. Gardie decided to go to France to seek help from his father. (It is possible that he was actually being deported: President Adams had just prepared a list of undesirable aliens who were to be forcibly returned to France.)

As the hour of departure approached, Gardie found himself unable to face even a temporary separation from his beautiful wife. She refused to accompany him. They were living in New York at the time, in a French boarding house which (on the authority of both Dunlap and Durang) can be identified as Fraunces' Tavern, the famous inn where, fifteen years earlier, George Washington had taken farewell of his officers. It is, of course, still standing today, at the corner of Broad and Pearl streets.

Early on the morning of July 20, 1798, the half-crazed Gardie, clutching a carving knife, crept upstairs to the small third-story room where his wife and the boy were sleeping. He stabbed her just once. Her dying screams awakened the child, who fled for help. No one would believe his frightful story. Too terrified to go back upstairs, he slipped into bed with one of the servants. At daybreak the two bodies were discovered: Anna Gardie lying as if quietly asleep, with a single wound in her breast, and her husband crumpled on the floor in a welter of blood, where he had thrust the knife into his own chest again and again.

In Boston and Savannah, Newport and New Orleans, every newspaper carried the story of the murdered ballerina. Perhaps on moonlit nights her ghost still dances in the splendid old building where she died.

—*New York Herald Tribune,* June 16, 1963

Anne Lecomte. (Harvard Theatre Collection)

VIII: *La Fille mal Gardée* in America

LA FILLE MAL GARDÉE, in Frederick Ashton's witty and handsome new version, enjoyed a resounding success in major American cities as one of the most important novelties in the repertoire of Britain's Royal Ballet during their 1961 tour of the States. The dazzling performances of its stars, Nadia Nerina, David Blair, Alexander Grant and Stanley Holden, brought them new laurels. Ashton's choreography, first seen at the Royal Opera House, Covent Garden, the year before (January 28, 1960), is entirely original, but it follows the libretto devised by Jean Dauberval nearly two centuries ago. The simple little story (girl finally gets the right boy) is just as appealing now as it was in 1789. Although the Ashton work may have provided many spectators with their first glimpse of a ballet which has been danced from Peru to Siberia, *La Fille mal Gardée* has been a perennial favorite in the United States.

Before it had been produced at the Paris Opéra, and before the Hérold and Hertel scores were written, *La Fille mal Gardée* had delighted American balletomanes. There is a possibility that they may even have seen it in the eighteenth century. At any rate, it has been presented intermittently in the United States for well over one hundred years, with such distinguished artists as Fanny Elssler, Anna Pavlova, Irina Baronova and Alicia Alonso dancing the role of Lise. The most recent production, by the American Ballet Center company, had its première on February 1, 1960 (following by just four days the London première of Ashton's version); the earliest may have taken place in 1794.

A "new Comic Pastoral Ballet, composed by Mr. Francis, called *L'Amour trouve les Moyens,* or THE FRUITLESS PRECAUTION" was given at the New Theatre, Philadelphia, on May 16, 1794. Since the titles *La Précaution Inutile* and (in Russia) *The Vain Precaution* have often served as alternates for *La Fille mal Gardée,* the similarity here, combined with a general description ("Comic Pastoral Ballet") which would certainly be applicable, suggests that this may have been a version of the popular classic.

William Francis, the choreographer who staged it, had been a favourite in London, Manchester, Liverpool and Dublin. It was the success of his pantomime *The Enchanted Wood,* given at the Haymarket Theatre, London, in 1792, that had earned him his invitation to Philadelphia. He might well have seen Dauberval's London production of *La Fille mal Gardée* in 1791.

Ballerina of *The Fruitless Precaution* was the mysterious Mme. Anna Gardie, who had made her American debut three weeks earlier in the ballet-pantomime *La Forêt Noire.* Very little is known about this beautiful and accomplished French dancer, although she was advertised in Philadelphia as "from the Theatre at Paris." Four years later, in New York, she was brutally murdered by her husband.

Making his first American appearance in *The Fruitless Precaution* was a certain Mons. Bellona, who is even more mysterious than Mme. Gardie. At later performances he was usually billed as "Bologna." This is a name celebrated in the annals of Pantomime. Could "Bellona," who often played Pantaloon in Philadelphia that season, have been the Bologna who later danced at the Theatre Royal, Covent Garden? When the latter died in 1805, it was said that "As a Pantaloon in Harlequinades, L. BOLOGNA excelled all his contemporaries." Such a dancer-mime would, of course, have made a wonderful simpleton.

Unfortunately the newspaper announcements, the only records of *The Fruitless Precaution* that have survived, do not list the characters, only the names of the dancers who appeared. The others were Messrs. Blissett, Darley, jun., Master T. Warrell and Mrs. De Marque. The ballet was repeated on May 16 and June 2, 1794. Incidentally, Bellona-Bologna danced in America only this one season, disappearing (perhaps to return to London and fame) after the theatre closed in July.

In the absence of definite proof that *The Fruitless Precaution* was a version of the same ballet, the production of *The Lovers, or La Fille mal Gardée* at the Lafayette Theatre, New York, on July 31, 1828, must be considered the American première. "A charming ballet, full of spirit and finesse, which . . . has obtained here a complete and merited success," commented "Ferdinand," the perceptive and well-informed critic of *Le Courrier des Etats-Unis.* "The plot is simple, but the curiosity of the spectator is excited and sustained by pleasant and gracious details, piquante and interesting situations. The talent with which this ballet has been reproduced should establish here, on a solid foundation, the reputation which M. Léon has justly acquired in the principal theatres of France."

Arnaud Léon, nearing fifty when he arrived in New York in 1828, certainly came to America with a background of enormous experience. Trained by Deshayes at the Paris Opéra, he had been a soloist there from 1801 to 1810, when he went to Russia to work under Didelot. After many appearances in the provincial theatres of France, where he often staged *La Fille mal Gardée,* he and his wife, Virginia Corby Léon (favourite partner of Carlo Blasis) had served from 1821 to 1826 as *Maestri di perfezione* at the ballet school at La Scala, Milan.

"Old Léon, the ballet master, was truly a character and quite *au fait* in his business," wrote Charles Durang, remembering him in later years. "His nose was ever covered with snuff. He took a pinch before the public while doing a pirouette."

Past his prime as a dancer, Léon did not appear in *La Fille mal Gardée* in New York. Lise was danced by Estelle Bernardin, a twenty-two-year-old ballerina who had made a promising debut at the Paris Opéra two years earlier, but for some reason had not been permanently engaged there. A pupil of Albert and Coulon, she was both pretty and accomplished.[1] "Mlle. Estelle has demonstrated strength, grace and lightness," commented the *Courrier des Etats-Unis.* "She is certainly a dancer of merit. Some people have found her dancing a little too jumpy (*sautillée*), but it should be remembered that her physique dictates the style which she follows; it is that of Mme. Montessu, *première danseuse* of the Opéra.

Colin was danced by Bertrand Benoni, who had worked under Blache in Bordeaux and Jean Petipa in Brussels. "Benoni was a small man, but did some astonishing things in dancing," said Charles Durang, while the *Courrier des Etats-Unis* admired his expressive pantomime. August Feltman was the unsuccessful suitor, called Nicaise in this production. His comic dancing was highly praised. Estelle Bernardin, in her role of Lise, was called upon to despise him; in reality, her feelings must have been quite the opposite, for she married him during this American tour.

By a miraculous chance, the actual orchestral parts used at this American première have survived (in a battered condition which testifies to their hard use) and are now in the Dance Collection of the New York Public Library. They bear Benoni's autograph signature and the musicians have added many little notes in various languages: *"Attendez jusqu'à ce qu'elle frappe sur l'épaule," "finisee di bere,"* and "Till curtain falls." Ivor Guest has identified this score as a version of the original used in Dauberval's first production in Bordeaux.

P.H. Hazard, known as the teacher of Mary Ann Lee and Augusta Maywood, was the next choreographer to produce *La Fille mal Gardée* in America. He presented it in Philadelphia on November 21, 1838, with Joséphine Stéphan (later well known in England as Mme. Petit-Stéphan) as Lise, and himself as Colin. Stéphan had a personal success, and the *Public Ledger* reported: "There is, independent of the scientific quality and brilliant execution of her dancing, an ease, and grace, and poetry of movement about her, that is always pleasing . . . In the *pas de deux* with Mons. Hazard, in the first act, the attitudes were difficult, excellent and even astonishing, and received generous bursts of applause. Mons. Hazard is a muscular and elastic dancer, scientific and very graceful; his *pirouettes* are remarkably fine . . ." The company as a whole, however, was not a very good one. After a few weeks of performances it disbanded; Mlle. Stéphan accepted an engagement in New York, and Hazard resumed his teaching.

Another graduate of the Paris Opéra, Mme. Anne Lecomte, made the role of Lise one of the triumphs of her long career. Her brother, Jules Martin, staged *La Fille mal Gardée* when they presented it at the Park Theatre, New York, on May 4, 1839. The *Spirit of the Times* described it as "an extremely pretty thing, — a little rustic, true-love tale of sunny France, told in *action,* not words, with perfect distinctness, and with pointed effect . . . There is full scope in the ballet for [Lecomte's] brilliant dancing . . . She cannot raise her arm or turn her head, without impressing you by her most gracious mien, and she falls into attitudes so easy and elegant . . . that your senses are charmed with the repose and beauty of the pictures she presents . . . Why cannot the ballet be attached permanently to our theatres?"

Probably the greatest Lise America has ever seen was the incomparable Fanny Elssler. She danced the role twice in Havana, Cuba, but only once, apparently, in the United States. This was at her farewell performance, and she gave only the second act! Her two-year-long American tour was already over, and she was busy getting ready to return to Europe, when she consented to make one final appearance at the Park Theatre, New York, on July 1, 1842, at a special benefit for the "Fund for the relief and support of Decayed Artists." The programme opened with the second act of *La Fille mal Gardée,* probably staged by Jules Martin, who played Mother Simone (although with his sister, Mme. Lecomte, he had danced Colin). In the earlier American productions, the role of Mme. Simone does not seem to have been given any particular prominence. Lise, Colin, and the simpleton — usually called Nicaise — were the important roles. Martin, however, made Madame Simone a featured part.

Unfortunately the New York critics have left us no description of Elssler's Lise. The *New York Daily Express*, commenting on the brilliant and crowded house and the star's charming little speech of farewell, simply said. "The heat was oppressive, but it seemed to have no effect on the peerless Fanny."

Although Caroline Dimier danced Lise in New York in 1847, and Hippolyte Monplaisir produced the ballet in New Orleans the following year, *La Fille mal Gardée* was largely forgotten until Anna Pavlova brought it to the Manhattan Opera House on April 15, 1914, in a production credited to Dauberval, "arranged by P. Zailich." The cast was a splendid one, with Enrico Cecchetti as the Mother, Laurent Novikoff as Colin, and Markowski as the despised suitor. The *New York Times* praised the ballet enthusiastically, and particularly admired Pavlova's deft and delicate comedy, although it had reservations about Novikoff's Colin.

In spite of the fact that Lise gave her such a rewarding role, Pavlova does not seem to have liked the ballet well enough to dance it often in America. It was occasionally given at matinées in 1914; and although it was scheduled for performances at the Manhattan Opera House in 1923, and listed in her souvenir programme for 1924-25, Pavlova seems to have cancelled these plans for reviving it.

It was Pavlova's famous partner, Mikhail Mordkin, who next staged *La Fille mal Gardée* in America. His version, which utilized the Hertel score plus a number of anonymous interpolations, was first danced by the Mordkin Ballet in Flint, Michigan, on October 13, 1937. Lucia Chase, who later became director of the American Ballet Theatre, was Lise, and Mordkin himself played the Mother, whom he called Marcelline. In spite of the gusto with which Mordkin attacked his role, *La Fille mal Gardée* was not received with unqualified enthusiasm when he gave it in New York the following season. "The old work has not been performed here for a great many years," wrote John Martin, "and apparently the reason for its resurrection now is that the role of the old woman, Marcelline, provides M. Mordkin with a good comedy part. Unhappily, this is almost all that can be said for the present revival . . . Except for Mordkin's zest and a *pas de trois* by the truly delightful Karen Conrad, Nina Stroganova and Leon Varkas, it was pretty inept . . ."

When the American Ballet Theatre decided to present *La Fille mal Gardée*, in its very first season, the choreography was entrusted to Bronislava Nijinska. She went over the score with Miss Chase and Dimitri Romanoff, who had danced Colin in the Mordkin Ballet, and they reviewed the pantomimic action as he had staged it (including the famous scene where Lise imagines herself with a family of growing children, which Karsavina showed to Frederick Ashton for the Royal Ballet production). Nijinska, remembering something of the St. Petersburg version, eliminated the music which had been interpolated in the Hertel score and restaged the dances in her own choreography. This version, lively and amusing, with several enchanting dances and a delightful atmosphere of the period, has remained in the repertoire of the American Ballet Theatre since January 19, 1940, although it has not been given every season. It has undergone several changes of title, being presented sometimes as *Naughty Lisette* and sometimes as *The Wayward Daughter*. Under its original title, *La Fille mal Gardée*, it was danced in London when the American Ballet Theatre appeared at the Royal Opera House in 1953.

Patricia Bowman, Ballet Theatre's first Lise, was a perfect soubrette, light, delicate, charming in every situation. Irina Baronova, who danced the role in 1941-42, brought a more robust humour, a broader style, and a fabulous technique which encompassed the most smooth pirouettes imaginable. The gifted character dancer Yurek Shabelevski was Ballet Theatre's original Colin, but the role did not suit him particularly well, and he soon ceded it to Dimitri Romanoff. The first Alain (the butterfly-chasing suitor) was Alexis Mendez Kosloff, whose bouncing leaps and ingratiatingly stupid grin are still memorable. He was succeeded by Ian Gibson, whose elevation was even more breath-taking. Neither Edward Caton nor Simon Semenoff, as Mother Simone, penetrated beyond the obvious low comedy possibilities of the role. It remained for Fernand Nault, who took it over in 1953, to discover its subtleties and polish its amusing detail.

While the American Ballet Theatre was in Mexico City in 1942, Anton Dolin arranged an excerpt from its production of *La Fille mal Gardée*, with Baronova in the title-role, and incorporated it in the Spanish-language film, *Yolanda*.

In 1949, Nana Gollner danced Lise in the first televised performance of *Fille*, which was also the television début of the American Ballet Theatre. Janet Reed, Ruth Ann Koesun and Lupe Serrano have all brought their distinctive qualities to the leading role, but its finest interpreter, in the Ballet Theatre production, has been Alicia Alonso. Her Lise has wit, style, a flair for comedy enhanced by a superb sense of timing, and, of course, a nearly flawless technique to support it.

Early in 1960, Fernand Nault staged the most recent version of *La Fille mal Gardée* for Robert Joffrey's American Ballet Center company. Using the Hertel score, he based his production on that of Nijinska, incorporating much of the pantomimic action she had devised. The ensemble dances were entirely restaged, however, and he added two solo *varia-tions* for the *premier danseur*. This version of *La Fille* was recently seen on a tour which extended all the way from Waltham, Massachusetts (where the première took place) to San Francisco. Ann Barzel saw it in Evanston, Illinois, and wrote in the *Chicago American:* ". . . *Fille mal Gardée* . . . was staged by Ballet Theatre's Fernand Nault and retains the charm of that company's version. Rochelle Zide in the title role was a smash hit both as comedienne and technician. Miss Zide, once of Ballet Russe, has always shown potentialities and this was the realization. [Jonathan] Watts danced the pleasant peasant who woos the maid. Paul Sutherland left the audience breathless when he bounded after butterflies as the slightly daft son of a rich man."

At other performances, Gerald Arpino danced Colin, with Françoise Martinet as Mother Simone.

The qualities which have kept Dauberval's ballet alive for nearly two centuries—its sharply defined characters, its amusing situations, its de-licious humour, and the ample opportunities it affords for brilliant dancing—have earned an enthusiastic reception for *La Fille mal Gardée* almost every time it has been produced in America. Its recurrent popular-ity in the United States furnishes substantial proof of its universal appeal.

—Contributed to *La Fille mal Gardée* (edited by Ivor Guest), 1960.

[1] For most of my information about Estelle Bernardin, I am indebted to Mme. Sylvie Chevally.

Paul and Amelie Galster Taglioni. (Dance Collection, The New York
Public Library)

IX: A Dancer's Odyssey: Paul and Amelie Taglioni

IN THE YEAR 1839 Paul Taglioni was at the height of his fame. He was just thirty-one years old. He held an excellent permanent position as first dancer and ballet master at the Berlin Royal Opera. His wife, Amelie Galster Taglioni, was *première danseuse*. They had danced together in Paris and London and most of the cities of the continent. The fame of Paul's sister Marie, who was acknowledged to be the greatest dancer in the world, lent a glamour to the very name of Taglioni. Foreign engagements were plentiful, whenever Paul and Amelie could get away from Berlin. There, they were secure in the favor of the King and his court.

And then, one evening, Paul chanced to read a copy of the Parisian journal *La Presse*. He was struck by a description of the new steamboat service which had just been inaugurated between Liverpool and New York. At that time, nearly a century ago, the old clipper ships were still the accepted means of ocean travel. The idea of a transatlantic voyage by steamer was as romantic and adventurous as a crossing by plane or

Zeppelin would be today. (*This was written in 1942. —I.G.*) It held a tremendous appeal for Taglioni.

As he went about his usual duties at the Berlin Opera, he tried to forget his fantastic desire to visit the United States. America was remote and perhaps uncivilized; it was said that wild red Indians were still plentiful, even in the eastern parts of the country. How would the natives of this strange land receive a classic dancer? The idea was absurd, and yet he could not forget it. It became an obsession. After all, was not his sister Marie at that very moment enjoying unprecedented triumphs in Russia, which also had been considered a barbaric hinterland?

At that time there was in London a bookseller named Seguin, who managed to combine the activities of a theatrical agent with his literary existence. He had already procured for Paul Taglioni several lucrative engagements at the King's Theatre in London. Now Taglioni wrote asking if he could arrange a tour to America. Seguin's reply was prompt and enthusiastic. Messrs. Price and Simpson, directors of the Park Theatre in New York, were in London. They were anxious to engage a celebrated dancer or two — (as a matter of fact, they were already angling for Fanny Elssler, whom they finally secured in 1840) — and the name of Taglioni would carry great weight in the United States. Would Paul and his wife consent to an engagement at the Park?

Highly elated, Taglioni hurried to the office of Baron Redern, director of the Opera. It would be necessary to obtain a prolonged leave of absence from Berlin, for the journey to America was long and arduous, even when it was accomplished by steamer. Not until the King himself had tried to dissuade Taglioni from leaving Germany was the furlough finally granted. The contract was signed at once, and sent back to Price and Simpson, who were waiting for it in London.

What a bustle of preparation then began! Taglioni and his wife were to travel alone, but they were obliged to take trunkloads of costumes and accessories with them. They must be prepared to present four full-length ballets, and innumerable divertissements. Ballet slippers were particularly important; where would they find anyone to make them if they should run short in the wilds of North America? A new wardrobe for Monsieur; ball dresses and formal toilettes for Madame, who would surely be feted in this strange country. Then music and orchestrations and all the variegated properties of a ballet company, even though this one consisted of only two persons.

Their farewell performance in Berlin was set for the evening of March 23. Paul Taglioni's own ballet *Don Quixote* was performed. Between the acts the King of Prussia himself came backstage to congratulate the dancers and wish them *bon voyage*. This royal visit was almost too much for the emotional artists; they began to regret their decision to leave Berlin, but now it was too late to change their minds.

On the following morning Paul and Amelie Taglioni began a journey which was to last until the sixth of May—six and a half weeks—and which was to employ almost every means of transportation then in existence. From Berlin to Zehlendorf they travelled by train, which also was something of a novelty. There they took leave of a friend who had accompanied them from Berlin. At Zehlendorf they took a stage-coach which carried them through Potsdam and across Germany to Frankfurt-am-Main. There a river boat took them down the Main and up the Rhine to Rotterdam, where they changed to a channel boat for London. There had been delays, and on reaching London they found their agent, Seguin, desperately afraid that they would miss the last mail coach to Liverpool. He hurried them through the customs, facilitating the inspection of their bulky and suspicious-looking trunks of theatrical accessories. A dash across London, and they just caught the stage, an express coach which galloped furiously through the night to Manchester. There they found once more the modern luxury of a railroad train, which carried them the remaining thirty-odd miles to Liverpool. In the latter city the Taglionis were much impressed by a railroad tunnel 4,000 feet long.

They had arrived just in time for the steamer. A violent storm was raging as they boarded the little boat which was to take them out to the *Great Liverpool*. The inclement weather did not prevent the citizens of the town from staging a gala farewell at the departure of the steamer. It seems to have resembled the launching of a liner like the *Queen Mary*. Throngs of people lined the shore, waving handkerchiefs; pennants and streamers fluttered from the masts of the smaller boats in the harbor; beautiful young girls, dressed all in white (in spite of the storm!) sang farewell songs.

In the midst of all this gaiety Paul and Amelie, desperately homesick, clung to each other and wished themselves back in Berlin. The desolate sight of the mast of a wrecked ship, which protruded warningly above the waves near the entrance of the harbor, did little to reassure them. As soon as they reached the open Atlantic, Paul became wretchedly seasick. He was forced to retire to his cabin and remain there for most of the voyage. Amelie was little affected by the sea; she soon became the center of social activity on board, charming all her fellow-passengers with her blonde German beauty, leading all the balls, and enlivening the dinners. The only thing which worried her was the impossibility of practicing; after all it would be no easy matter for a classic dancer to make a debut in a strange country after six weeks of inactivity! Paul was too ill to care very much; he might not live to reach New York anyway.

Like most seasickness, his indisposition finally passed, and he ventured out on deck, a little green about the gills, but otherwise cheerful enough. The passengers were so surprised at the sight of a strange face that they asked Captain Fayrer if he had been rescued from the sea! But the adventures of the voyage were not over. An Englishman who occupied the cabin directly opposite that of the Taglionis was even more seriously ill than Paul had been. The ship's doctor had been attending him regularly, and one day he startled everyone by announcing that his patient had smallpox! The entire population of the ship was thrown into consternation. Luckily there was preventive serum on board, and everyone who was willing to submit to the operation was vaccinated. Taglioni and his wife both consented, and were saved much inconvenience when the ship reached New York, for those who had refused were held in quarantine for many days.

Later, James Gordon Bennett, in his highly individual journal, the *New York Weekly Herald,* made good copy of the vaccination incident. He described how the Taglionis, with their imperfect English, failed to understand what the doctor wanted of them, and how Madame believed that he wished to search her trunks for smuggled goods. Then, when he mentioned arms, Paul thought he meant firearms.

"Arms! Mon Dieu! We have no several arms," Paul is quoted as saying, "No arms, Monsieur! No pistole! No dagger! No noseing of some arms — Mon Dieu! I have no arms — Madame has no arms!"

The doctor remarked that they seemed to have very good arms, and legs too.

"Legs! —*Comprend pas.* Ah, *oui!* But you must not search my legs — nor my wife's legs. We shall live by our legs."

This colorful episode probably existed principally in the imagination of Bennett or his informant. At any rate, the vaccination had such a serious effect on poor Paul that he was taken ill again, and did not reach New York in the best of spirits.

It was on a glorious moonlight night that the *Great Liverpool,* after a journey of seventeen days, arrived in New York harbor. There were no skyscrapers on the horizon then; New York was a charming little town with pretty shaded walks and attractive small shops and theatres. The Battery, with its lovely green trees and grass, was the favorite promenade of fashionable society. The *Great Liverpool* docked there, and the Taglionis had simply to walk across Broadway to reach the exclusive Globe Hotel. This excellent establishment, which had been highly recommended by their fellow passengers, was run by a certain M. Blancard, former master chef to Napoleon.

As soon as he set foot on firm land again, Paul recovered from his indisposition. Eager to get to work at once, he went next morning to call on his directors, Price and Simpson, at the Park Theatre. As he walked up Broadway he noticed, with his Italian eye for beauty, that the American women were almost universally pretty, and exquisitely dressed. The men did not win his approval; he saw too many of them straddling the balustrades at the entrances to cafes and saloons, informally reading their gigantic newspapers and spitting tobacco juice on the pavement. Later he noticed that at the theatre the occupants of the upper boxes did not hesitate to dangle their legs over the railings, until those seated below objected loudly to this obstruction of their vision. Just a barbarous American custom!

It was decided that the Taglionis should make their debut in the famous ballet *La Sylphide,* favorite vehicle of Paul's sister, Marie. It had never been presented in America in its entirety, although other dancers had already given individual excerpts from it. The classic ballet was rapidly attaining a position of great popularity in the American theatre. It had been introduced in 1827 by a French dancer, Madame Hutin, whose revealing flesh-colored tights so scandalized the conservative and somewhat provincial Americans that she was requested to wear pantalettes at all future performances! During the intervening twelve years, however, the ballet had been firmly established in popular favor, and several excellent artists, such as Madame Augusta, Madame Celeste, and Madame Lecomte (future employer of Marius Petipa , during his brief visit to America in the autumn of 1839) had appeared before the American public. As yet, however, no first-class male dancer had appeared here. The dancing of Paul Taglioni came as a revelation.

The preparation of *La Sylphide* was not an easy matter. There were very few trained dancers in New York, and Taglioni was forced to recruit a *corps de ballet* from whatever material he could find at hand. The ensemble must have been distinctly bad; all the critics attacked the poor girls with bitterness, one gentleman finding them "a dull, dowdy set of unfashionable mimics." "Nothing will draw so uniformly, just now, as dancing and music," protested another, "and we trust that the public will not rest satisfied till there shall be attached to one of our theatres an excellent *corps de ballet.*"

The miracle is that Paul Taglioni was able to present anything as complicated as *La Sylphide* at all. He worked hard all day long, and finally whipped something into shape. The first performance was set for May 21, and a tremendous crowd collected at the theatre on that night. They were met with the announcement that because of the indisposition of M. Taglioni, the opening of *La Sylphide* was postponed until the following evening. Was his vaccination still bothering him, or had he eaten too well of M. Blancard's Napoleonic cooking, or was it simply overwork? Whatever it was, the illness was not serious, and by the next day he had recovered. On Wednesday, May 22, Paul and Amelie Taglioni made their American debut at the Park Theatre, in *La Sylphide*.

Paul and Amelie Taglioni were the rage of New York. Balletomanes avidly compared their virtues with those of the few classic dancers who had preceded them to America. To be sure, Madame Taglioni was not as good a mime as Celeste or Augusta, but she was a far better dancer. And as for Monsieur! There really was nothing with which to compare him. There was M. Martin, of course, the brother and partner of Madame Lecomte. He was remarkably graceful, but technically he could not even approach Paul Taglioni. Nothing remotely resembling Paul's leaps and pirouettes and other *tours de force* had ever been seen in America. Besides, he had a symmetrical figure and remarkably well-shaped legs, which did much to lessen the American prejudice against male dancers.

The pair had made their debut at the Park Theatre on May 22, 1839, in *La Sylphide*. The unexpected postponement of the opening, originally scheduled for the previous evening, served only to whet the appetites of the audience. They were received with an enthusiasm which was shared by pit, gallery, and critics alike; even the manager was observed to smile, for the first time in months. His usually empty house was crowded at last!

"Madame Taglioni is a fair-haired, German-looking lady, of a tall and elegant shape, very pretty but not very beautiful," commented the *Spirit of the Times*. "Her husband is Italian in appearance, wondrously well formed—limbs clean and sinewy like those of a race-horse, with a face which reminds you of the pictures of his famous sister, particularly about the mouth.

"The two combined, present the highest attraction we have ever had in the ballet. The style of Mme. Taglioni . . . is quite simple, —every *appearance* of exertion is avoided in the execution, and nothing is attempted, which would *seem* to require great muscular effort. Her dancing speaks to you . . . in the language of sentiment. In observing her, you have revealed to you what those writers from abroad mean by 'the poetry of motion.' She flits around the stage like a true fairy, her tenderness for her mortal lover is visible in every attitude, and joy, and hope, fear and despair, alike find expression . . . ."

From the examination of other contemporary criticisms, whose language is vague and pretty and not at all definite, it seems that the particular *forté* of the Taglionis lay in their exquisite execution of *pas de deux,* and especially in adagio movements. They introduced feats that had never been seen before, and audiences never ceased to marvel at the length of time that Amelie could sustain a difficult pose. The two had danced together for years, and had attained a perfect unison and delicate finish. Paul's solo work seems to have been more striking than that of Amelie, for he had a great deal of facility in the execution of startling feats, but her ethereal grace, which must have resembled that of her sister-in-law Marie, found its admirers among the connoisseurs.

In the *Weekly Herald* James Gordon Bennett remarked the great change that had taken place in the public attitude towards the art of the ballet, since its introduction in 1827.

"In every pirouette the graceful Taglioni almost reveals every lineament of her beautiful form," he wrote, "yet hardly an improper throb passes through the imagination of any present at the Park.

". . . The ballet of the *Sylphide* creates in our minds a species of poetical ethereal enthusiasm, which is a part of the deep throb of virtue itself. A beautiful young lady— educated and accomplished—who relishes the refined movements of the Taglionis, gives an evidence, not only of the purity of her heart and imagination, but of the strength of her principles, and the power of a lofty intellect. These Taglionis are very superior artists."

Until the end of May, Paul and Amelie danced *La Sylphide* almost every night. On the first of June, they introduced *Le Bal Masqué*, a divertissement from the opera *Gustavus III*. This was a favorite production with dancers of that day. It seems to have been an elastic sort of concoction, into which each dancer introduced his own favorite numbers. The Taglionis chose as their contributions to the potpourri two character duets, a *Pas Hongrois* and a *Pas Styrien*.

Between their own performances, Paul and Amelie found time to pay frequent visits to Delmonico's Cafe, a popular and cosmopolitan resort where they reencountered many of their acquaintances from the *Great Liverpool*. Among these was an Italian theatrical agent, Signor Bergonzio, who undertook to arrange for them a brief tour of the eastern coast.

For diversion the Taglionis (in typical professional style) attended the theatre. They particularly admired the great American tragedian Edwin Forrest, and found much to learn from his eloquent pantomime in the last act of *Richard III*. They did not care so much for the production of *The Dumb Girl of Portici,* and found it quite comical to see the supposed Neapolitans boxing in a typically American manner.

The Taglionis ended their first New York engagement on June 3, when a performance was given for the benefit of Madame Taglioni, with the special attraction of a double bill consisting of both *La Sylphide* and *Le*

Bal Masqué. In spite of a severe rainstorm the house was crowded with admirers who had come to pay homage to the pretty German ballerina and her talented husband.

From New York Paul and Amelie travelled to Baltimore and Philadelphia. In the former city they found an ensemble so crude and inexperienced that while Paul was dancing his *pas seul* they strolled out on the stage, seated themselves comfortably on the floor, and proceeded to smoke cigarettes (this in 1839!) while they watched the performance! In Philadelphia, however, they were agreeably surprised to find a better *corps de ballet* than had been available in New York. At that time there was a very good dancing teacher in Philadelphia, a Frenchman named Hazard. One of his pupils, Augusta Maywood, was so accomplished that with only one year of additional study abroad she was able to make a successful debut at the Paris Opéra. Another, Mary Ann Lee, was the first native American ballerina to tour the United States as a full-fledged "star."

The Taglionis opened in Philadelphia on June 10, and gave five performances at the Chestnut Street Theatre. Their programs there consisted of the second act of *La Sylphide* (the Philadelphians felt cheated at not seeing the whole ballet) and two divertissements, the *Pas Styrien* and a solo *Cachucha* by Amelie. Philadelphians liked *La Sylphide,* and nearly spoiled the lovely adagio by applauding so frantically in the middle of it that the dancers could hardly hear the music, but they found the *Cachucha* entirely too bold and energetic for a lady. It probably just didn't suit the blonde and etherial Amelie, for in the following year, when the dazzling Fanny Elssler gave them the same dance, Philadelphia (and all the rest of the country!) was completely captivated.

Returning to New York, the Taglionis began their second engagement at the Park Theatre on June 17. On the twenty-first they made a bold stroke for attention with the production of Auber's *Le Dieu et la Bayadère.* This popular opera-ballet had already been danced in New York City by Celeste and Augusta and Lecomte, so that the balletomanes had plenty of opportunity to make comparisons. The Taglionis introduced one striking novelty when they converted the famous *Shawl Dance,* traditionally executed by the ballerina alone, into a *pas de deux.* The fact that Paul's presence completely spoiled the meaning of the number, which was supposed to be a dance of seduction, did not make much difference either to the artists or their audiences. So long as the dance was beautiful—and it evidently was—nothing else mattered.

Another new ballet, *Undine, ou La Naiade,* made its appearance on the first of July. This production of Paul Taglioni's should not be confused with the more famous *Ondine* created by Perrot for Fanny Cerrito in London in 1843. The themes were similar, both concerning water spirits, but the choreography of the two ballets was entirely different.

With the beginning of July the heat in New York had become unbearable. In spite of the popularity of the Taglionis and their new productions, audiences were becoming thin and listless. At the request of Price and Simpson, who wished the Taglionis to play a return engagement at a more favorable season, Paul had already written to Berlin for permission to prolong his stay in America. While awaiting for a reply, he decided that it might be interesting to see something of the United States besides its stage doors. The fashionable resorts were Saratoga and Niagara Falls, so the Taglionis resolved to visit them.

In Brooklyn they boarded the steamer *Albany*, which actually had three decks! The Taglionis were much impressed. In this palatial vessel they travelled up the Hudson, whose scenery they found to be the most romantic and picturesque in the world, although but three months before they had made a similar journey up the Rhine. They stopped off at West Point to see the Military Academy and the white marble statute of Kosziusko. At Albany they took a stagecoach (drawn by *four* horses, another extravagance which impressed the European travellers) to Saratoga, which they found as pleasantly civilized as any of the famous German spas. Martin Van Buren, President of the United States, visited Saratoga during the same month, so they were in distinguished company.

On the edge of a forest near Rochester the Taglionis had a thrilling glimpse of some Indians in their native dress. The sight of a herd of wild buffalo, in a clearing, was even more exciting. Later they saw an Indian woman, by the roadside, working busily at handwork, while several children swarmed around her. They stopped and bought souvenirs for their friends in Berlin: work-boxes, little wicker baskets, and deer-skin moccasins decorated with colorful bead-work.

To the Taglionis, Lake Ontario seemed as limitless as an ocean. When they were nearing the Falls, they were awed to hear the distant roar of the water and see clouds of steam rising far away. At Niagara they dressed up in absurd oil-cloth costumes and ventured into the grotto behind the falls. Paul was presented with an engraved certificate testifying that he had been under Niagara, and he was as proud of it as though it had been a gift from royalty. After a brief excursion across the border into Canada—just so they could boast that they had been there, probably—the dancers returned to New York by the shortest route. They were both homesick for news from Berlin.

Waiting in New York they found a thick packet of letters. Among them was the hoped-for permission to prolong their visit to America. On July 29 they began their third New York engagement, dancing *La Naiade* and a new comic *pas de deux,* the *Jota Aragonesa* from *Don Quixote.* When in August the Park Theatre closed for redecoration, they took advantage of the holiday to make brief appearances in Boston and Providence. The Boston visit was uneventful, the Providence one rather exciting. Providence was an extremely religious city, boasting no less than thirty churches for its 17,000 souls. One of these, an Anabaptist church, was located directly across the street from Shakespeare Hall, the theatre where the Taglionis were to appear. When Paul went down to the theatre for rehearsal, he saw a huge crowd gathered around the stage door. The object of their attention seemed to be a poster depicting Amelie Taglioni, in her *Sylphide* costume, floating in mid-air above a picturesque representation of the *Great Liverpool,* while Paul pursued her with outstretched arms. What we would not give to see a copy of this vanished poster! It must have been delectable.

At any rate, it was the subject of an oration which was being delivered by the minister of the Anabaptist church. "Dear children," he was pleading, "let us not be led into temptation! turn with abhorrence from this place of vice and corruption!" Here he pointed dramatically to the theatre. Just at this moment the stage manager stepped out and began a counter-attack. He described vividly the European and American triumphs of the Taglionis, and finished up with a rousing, "Step right up and take your tickets, ladies and gentlemen!"

Paul Taglioni decided that it might be wise to slip quietly away and return when the crowd had disappeared. He rather expected an exciting performance that evening.

Just before the ballet began, he peeped through the curtains to see how the audience was behaving. Every one of the boxes was full, and the upper balcony was crowded with standees, but the rest of the house — where the middle class people would ordinarily have been seated — was completely empty! Consequently there was no riot — the people who might have caused one had stayed at home. The worst disaster of the evening was the wretched playing of the exquisite violin solo which accompanied the *Sylphide* adagio. The most popular item on the program was the comic *Jota,* which had to be repeated, much to the disgust of Paul Taglioni, who thought this dance just a little vulgar, and certainly not representative of his best work.

Back in New York, the Taglionis busied themselves with rehearsals for another new ballet, *Nathalie, ou la Laitière Suisse,* which had been produced in Vienna by Filippo Taglioni, father of Paul and Marie, in 1821. The plot of this ballet hangs upon the uncanny resemblance between the hero and a statue. Unfortunately the Taglionis had not been able to bring with them, among their numerous other properties, a life-size statue of Paul. It was decided that the quickest way to make one was to make plaster casts of his face and body. For the facial mask, Taglioni went to a phrenologist who was experienced in the making of casts. The process was uncomfortable, to be sure, but he emerged from it unscathed. For the casts of his legs and torso, however, he entrusted himself to the ministrations of the chief property man at the theatre. Not until he was completely encased in plaster, and nearly suffocating to death, did he discover that the man was absolutely inexperienced, and had never made a cast in his life! It was finally necessary to use a hatchet to extricate Paul's precious legs, and he received several wounds. Miraculously, none of them were serious. They finally obtained a statue by less drastic methods.

In the meantime, a very talented dancer, Madame Proche-Giubelei, had arrived from Europe with her husband, a singer, to take part in the autumn season at the Park. She was recruited for *Nathalie,* in which there was an important *pas de trois,* the *Tyrolienne.* The first performance of the new ballet took place on September 12. On the same evening, Beethoven's *Fidelio* was presented. In order that the audience might have an extra glimpse of the new ballerina, a *pas de deux* for Madame Proche-Giubelei and Monsieur Taglioni was interpolated in the opera. Imagine the horror of the music critics, if Beethoven's masterpiece were treated in such debonair fashion today!

The Taglionis' leave of absence from the Berlin Opera was rapidly drawing to a close. They had actually booked passage on the *President,* but the popularity of their performances induced them to postpone their departure until the sailing of the *British Queen* on October 1. It was fortunate that they did so, for the *President,* largest super-steamer that had yet been built, sailed blithely away and was never heard from again.

On September 24 Paul and Amelie Taglioni appeared in New York for the last time. The farewell program, a benefit for Madame, consisted of the second act of *La Sylphide* and all of *Nathalie.* It was a triumph for both dancers, and a fitting conclusion to their pleasant sojourn in America.

On the eve of the sailing of the *British Queen,* Paul Taglioni took a last walk through the quiet city. As he passed a shop, he was suddenly attracted by the sight of his own name in the window. It was the phrenologist's, where he had had the life-mask made for *Nathalie.* And there in the window was a perfect reproduction of his skull, between those of two notorious murderers. To make matters worse, his showman's eye noted that their names were inscribed in red letters, fully as large as his!

So with bitter reflections upon the fame of an artist as compared with that of a criminal, Taglioni returned to the Globe Hotel for his last night in America. Next day the *British Queen* carried him and his wife back to Europe, where there awaited him a long and honorable career at the Berlin Opera. He truly lived for the stage and for his beloved ballet. He died on January 6, 1884, just three months after he had retired from active work in the theatre.

—American Dancer, March 1942

Playbill for November 9, 1839. (Harvard Theatre Collection)

X: The Petipa Family in Europe and America

JEAN PETIPA, father of the great choreographer of the Russian Ballet, was born in 1787. His name first enters theatrical history in the year 1815, when he was *premier danseur* at the Théâtre de la Porte Saint-Martin, in Paris. The *maître de ballet* of this house was Jean-Baptiste Blache, a famous choreographer who had produced at the Paris Opéra, in Bordeaux, Marseilles, and other French cities. It is probable that Blache trained Jean Petipa.

In September, 1815, the ballet company of the Porte Saint-Martin gave a series of twenty guest performances at the Monnaie, in Brussels. The principal dancers were Messieurs Petipa, Rhenon, and Pierson, and Mesdames Pierson, Darcourt, and Marinette. This was Jean Petipa's first appearance at the theatre with which he was to be associated for more than twenty years. At the close of their short engagement, the little troupe returned to Paris for their first season under the Restoration.

At about this time Jean married a young actress, who bore him three sons and a daughter. Of Jean, little is known. The daughter became an opera singer. Lucien was born in Marseilles in 1815, and Marius, the greatest of his family, was born in the same city on March 11, 1818.

In the meantime, the Monnaie decided to form a permanent corps de ballet. In 1816 its directors engaged several dancers, and the following year they added a staff ballet-master, Eugène Hus, who had danced at the Paris Opéra thirty years earlier. In 1819 a new director, Bernard, took charge of the affairs of the theatre. Retaining Hus, he decided to secure new dancers. He selected Mlle. Marie Lesueur, a nineteen-year-old Parisian girl, as *première,* Jean Petipa as *premier danseur,* and a Monsieur Desplaces as *deuxième danseur.* Madame Petipa was engaged as *jeune première* among the actresses. The corps de ballet at the Monnaie consisted, at this time, of ten *sujets*, or soloists, and an ensemble of twelve *danseuses*, twelve *danseurs*, and twelve children.

83

The three new dancers, Petipa, Desplaces, and Mlle. Lesueur, made their debuts together on May 20, 1819, in Blache's ballet *Almaviva et Rosine,* a reworking of Beaumarchais, which was used by Mozart as well as by Paisiello and Rossini. A few days later, the entire company moved to a magnificent new building which had just been completed. A gala was given to celebrate its opening, and on this occasion Petipa presented his first choreographic composition, a divertissement interpolated in Grétry's opera *La Caravane du Caire.* It won enthusiastic praise from the critics, and Petipa's position was assured.

The ballet repertoire at the Monnaie consisted mainly of classics, by Blache, Milon, Aumer, and Gardel, which had already been presented at Parisian theatres, and which Hus re-adapted for the Monnaie. Although engaged chiefly as dancer, Petipa soon became Hus's assistant, producing as many ballets as his master. On September 1, 1819, Petipa presented his first complete ballet, a production in one act, called *La Kermesse,* based on the National Flemish Carnival which indicated aspirations for Belgian independence.

On June 17, 1821, Petipa produced a work of major importance, the two-act ballet *La Naissance de Venus et de l'Amour.* Mlle. Lesueur danced the role of Venus, and little Lucien Petipa, then but five years old, took the part of Amour.

The celebrated painter Jacques Louis David was at that time a resident of Brussels. An ardent revolutionary and supporter of Napoleon, whom he painted several times, he had been exiled from France after Waterloo and the restoration of the Bourbons. David was very fond of the ballet, and with good reason. When he was a struggling young artist he had been engaged to assist Fragonard in painting the frescoes for the new house of the great dancer Marie Madeleine Guimard (1743-1816). She became interested in his work, and it is said that she paid for his studies before he won the Prix de Rome.

During his old age David, not forgetting the days when he costumed Talma, often attended the performances at the Monnaie. He lived very close to the theatre, and went so frequently that he had a certain seat always reserved. If for any reason he was absent or late, and someone else took that particular chair, a neighbor would politely inform the intruder it was especially reserved for M. David, and must remain empty unless he came.

He must have seen Jean Petipa dance often. At any rate, he was so deeply impressed by the ballet *La Naissance de Venus* that it inspired him to paint the picture *Mars Desarmé par Venus,*[1] which hangs in the Brussels Musée Ancien. Mlle. Lesueur served as model for the figure of

Venus, but a little servant girl posed for the feet of the goddess, as those of the hard-working ballerina were not sufficiently beautiful to please the painter. Young Lucien Petipa, a strikingly handsome child, posed for Amour. A subscriber of the Monnaie was Mars, while the central figure of the Three Graces was Mlle. Philippont, a dancer who had won the favor of the Prince of Orange. According to a letter written by David to the tenor Defosse, even Mars' helmet was a property of the theatre.

Although David probably began his picture shortly after the first production of the ballet in 1821, he did not complete it until three years later, for it bears the date 1824. David took particular pains with his Venus. In his original version the goddess faced front, but later he repainted the whole figure. As soon as the picture was finished, it was exhibited in Brussels for the benefit of the Old People's Home, and then shown in Paris, where it attracted considerable attention and brought the painter a profit of 45,000 francs. When David died in the following year, at the age of seventy-seven, *Mars Desarmé par Venus* passed to his son, and then to the City of Brussels.

In the meantime a new dancer, M. Benoni, made his debut at the Théâtre de la Monnaie on July 10, 1821, in *Les Jeux d'Eglé*. A *premier danseur*, he ranked below Jean Petipa. Remaining at the Monnaie for six seasons, he took leading roles in most of the productions. In 1823 he married Mlle. Feltmann, a *troisième danseuse* (who eventually replaced Mlle. Lesueur as *première*).

On February 24, 1822, Petipa produced *Monsieur Deschalumeaux,* an ambitious ballet in three acts, adapted from the work by Creuzé de Lesser and Gaveaux. Eugene Hus died in the same year, and Petipa became the official director of the ballet. At this time gas illumination was introduced.

The opening of the new season saw many changes in the company. Madame Petipa retired from the stage, and Mlle. Adeline, a promising young dancer who had been a soloist since 1819, was promoted to rank with Mlle. Lesueur as *première*. Petipa showed his progressive spirit by engaging many guest artists for individual performances. During 1823 M. Aniel, *premier danseur* of the Grand Théâtre of Bordeaux, M. Laurençon, *danseur comique,* and the celebrated Auguste Vestris made special appearances in Brussels. In 1824 Petipa continued this policy by engaging M. Télémaque, of the Porte Saint-Martin, to appear as Alexis in *Le Déserteur,* a famous old ballet by Dauberval. During 1823 and 1824 Petipa produced eleven new works by Gardel, Dauberval and Blache, but nothing of his own. In 1825, however, he created two ballets: *Frasac, ou la Double Noce,* on February 18, and *Le Cing Juillet,* on July 9. The music for both was composed by Joseph François Snel (1793-1861), a member of the staff of the Monnaie, with whom Petipa often collaborated.

Meanwhile the *première danseuse*, Mlle. Lesueur, had been the victim of a tragic accident. In January, 1825, during the general rehearsal of Blache's *Jenny, ou Le Mariage Secret;* she fell through a trap-door, narrowly escaping death. Although seriously injured, she forced herself to perform the next day. (The strain was too much, and she was obliged to rest for six weeks. On her re-appearance she danced so badly that she was hissed.) After struggling in vain against failing health, she finally retired and married M. van Gobbelschroy, Minister of the Interior under King William I.

In 1825 the corps de ballet was slightly enlarged, to include sixteen men, sixteen women, eight children, and six pupils, who occasionally appeared. The following season Petipa organized a regular conservatory of dancing, composed of twenty-four pupils. Lessons were given four times each week, and a yearly examination determined which pupils were qualified for the corps de ballet. It was in this school that Marius and Lucien, then aged eight and ten respectively, received their fine training.

Jean Petipa retired from the stage at this time, and was replaced by Benoni as *premier mime,* and Ragaine as *premier danseur.* Ragaine made his debut on May 11, 1826. In July and August a distinguished guest artist, Mme. Montessu, *première danseuse* of the Paris Opéra, made twelve appearances. For the last three she was joined by her husband. Petipa produced three ballets in 1826. *Monsieur de Porceaugnac,* with choreography by himself and music by Snel, had its premiere on February 5. The story was probably taken from Molière's play. On April 3 he gave Deshayes'[2] ballet *Zemir et Azor,* which was danced to music by Schneitzhoeffer, future composer of Taglioni's *La Sylphide,* and on December 14 he presented *Jocko, le Singe de Brésil.* This last ballet had already been created by Philippe Taglioni for his daughter Marie, but although Petipa, in Brussels, followed the same subject, he created his own choreography. On October 26, 1826, a memorial program called *Hommage à Talma* was given at the Monnaie in honor of the great tragedian, who had just died. Petipa arranged a special ballet divertissement for this performance.

In 1827 Petipa produced two ballets by Aumer, with music by Hérold: *Astolphe et Joconde,* and *La Somnambule.* Both of them had recently been created at the Paris Opéra. On February 22, he presented *Gulliver,* an adaptation of Swift's satire after the original by Coralli. During 1827 young Marius Petipa, aged nine, made his debut. None of its details are known. Perhaps he was a Lilliputian in *Gulliver!*

Jean Petipa was intent on making the ballet of the Théâtre de la Monnaie one of the finest in Europe. He was gradually strengthening his personnel, and in 1827 two new *premiers danseurs,* Leblond and Lasserre, and three new *premières,* Mmes. Martin and Leblond, and Mlle. Leroux, made their debuts. The last-named was probably the Pauline Leroux who later won distinction at the Paris Opéra. M. Lasserre made his debut in an old classic, *La Fille mal Gardée.* Among the guest artists who appeared were Mlles. Maria, Perceval, and Mimi Dupuis, all from the Paris Opéra, and the superb mime and character dancer Mazurier, who made a sensational success as Jocko, the Brazilian ape. This promising young artist died while he was still in his twenties.

In the same year a serious scandal upset the discipline of the ballet at the Monnaie. M. and Mme. Leblond accused the comic dancer Laurençon of the theft of 350 florins, declaring that he had robbed them in the foyer of the theatre itself, possibly during a rehearsal. Laurençon was arrested and condemned to a year in prison, but he appealed the case and was released. On his reappearance in *Deux bailles, ou les vendangeurs, (Two baskets, or the vintagers)* there was such an uproar of applause mingled with hisses and cat-calls that the police had to order the lowering of the curtain. The audience still refused to be quieted, and the commotion went on for fifteen minutes before people dispersed to continue the brawl at the well known Cafe Au Doux. After this unfortunate evening Laurençon was forced to leave Brussels. He was replaced by Girel, who made his debut in *Les Meuniers,* and later produced ballets of his own.

On February 18, 1828, Jean Petipa, presented one of his most successful compositions, in seven scenes, called *Les Petites Danaïdes.* The music was, as usual, by Snel. This was followed on August 7 by a revival of *La Naissance de Venus et de l'Amour,* in which Marius probably inherited his brother's role.

On August 2, 1830, Mme. Lecomte, who was later to bring Jean and Marius Petipa to America, made her debut as *première danseuse* in Sor's ballet *Cendrillon.* It was a troubled debut, for the Belgian national revolt was brewing.

Since the downfall of Napoleon and the Treaty of Vienna, in 1815, Belgium and Holland had been united under the rule of William I of Orange. It was an arrangement which did not in the least suit the liberty-loving Belgians. For some time discontent had been growing, and it was a performance at the Monnaie which marked the beginning of the Revolution.

On August 25, 1830, Auber's opera-ballet *La Muette de Portici* was presented, with Madame Benoni in the role of the dumb girl, Fenella. The story of *La Muette* is based upon historical fact, and deals with the uprising of the Neapolitans against their ruler, Alfonso, during the seventeenth century. It contains many inciting passages, and to oppressed Brussels it provided the spark which inflamed them to rebellion. During the third act, when Masaniello, leader of the Neapolitan people, shouted "To arms!," the audience rose en masse, re-echoing his cry. It was impossible to complete the performance. Screaming hysterically, the public poured out into the public square, where they were joined by a restless waiting throng unable to get into the theatre. Rioting broke out, the royal guard was attacked, and it retired, without resistance, to the Palace.

Next day a citizens' committee took over the government of Brussels. William I, not realizing the seriousness of the situation, sent his son, the Prince of Orange, to parley with the rebels. All attempts at negotiation failed, and fighting broke out all over Belgium, while volunteers poured into the capital to join the revolutionaries.

Meanwhile the theatre was closed for several weeks, Re-opening on September 12, it struggled through a week of performances given under the most difficult conditions; after the nineteenth, it was closed for good. The troops of Prince Frederic, William's second son, were approaching the city. They entered Brussels on September 23, but after three days of barricades the revolutionaries drove them out. On October 4 the provisional government in Brussels proclaimed the nation's independence.

While the fighting continued for some time, the revolutionary forces were eventually victorious, and in November the Monnaie was reopened. Petipa and his collaborator Snel celebrated the victory by the production, in January 1831, of a patriotic ballet bearing the odd title *Le 23, 24, 25 et 26 Septembre*. It commemorated the battle of Brussels, which had taken place during those days. The Monnaie's part in the outbreak of the revolution was further signalized by the striking of a medal, bearing on one side a picture of the theatre and the words *Muette de Portici, Bruzelles, XXV Aout MDCCCXXX*, and on the other a representation of a lion with the Belgian flag, and the words *Courage et Force, Independance, Révolution Belge 1830*.

At the end of the season, in July 1831, Jean Petipa left the Monnaie. It is interesting to speculate on the reasons for his departure. Although unlikely, in view of his patriotic productions, it is possible he was actually sympathetic to the Loyalist cause. His former *première*, Mlle. Lesueur, was married to one of the Ministers of William I, and Petipa's important position in an endowed theatre had brought him into close contact with court officials, A newcomer, M. Laffilé, assumed the directorship of the Monnaie in August, and perhaps he had his own reasons for changing ballet masters. At any rate, Petipa spent the next two years wandering through the provincial theatres of France, producing ballets in Lyon, Marseilles, and Bordeaux. His post in Brussels was taken over by M. Bartholomin, an ambitious young man who had joined the corps de ballet in 1824 as a *coryphé*, and gradually worked himself up to the post of assistant ballet master.[3]

In 1833 Jean Petipa returned to the Monnaie, where he shared with Bartholomin the post of *maître de ballet*, occasionally appearing on the stage in mimed roles, but producing no more ballets. In 1835 he returned to Bordeaux, where his work, especially *Les Petites Danaïdes,* enjoyed tremendous popularity.

During the period which followed, Petipa devoted much of his time and energy to the development of his sons, now old enough to be thinking about careers of their own. Marius made his professional debut —if one excepts those early appearances in Brussels —at the Comédie Française in 1838, when he danced a *pas de deux* with Carlotta Grisi at a performance given for the benefit of Mlle. Rachel. Soon after, he was engaged as *premier danseur* at Nantes where he choreographed *Le Droit du Seigneur, La Petite Bohemienne and La Noce à Nantes.* Lucien's more auspicious debut was made at the Paris Opéra on June 10, 1839.

In the summer of 1839 Jean Petipa's former *première* at Brussels, Mme. Lecomte, invited Jean and Marius Petipa to come to the United States, as ballet master and *premier danseur* of a ballet company she was organizing in New York. Mme. Lecomte had already danced in the United States for two seasons, and her success had been so encouraging that now she decided to bring over several European dancers. Her husband, a tenor who also appeared at the Monnaie, had retired from the stage to become her manager.

The Petipas sailed from London September 2, on the *British Queen.* They arrived in New York eighteen days later, just in time to witness the last performances of Paul and Amelie Taglioni, who were completing a four-months tour of Baltimore, Philadelphia, Boston and Providence as well as New York. Their farewell performance, a benefit for Madame Taglioni, took place on September 24. In all probability Marius and Jean Petipa were in the audience at the Park Theatre to watch *Nathalie, la Laitière Suisse,* and the second act of *La Sylphide.* The Taglionis went back to Europe on the return trip of the *British Queen,* sailing a few days later.

At this time Marius Petipa was barely twenty. During his recent engagement at Nantes he had stumbled during a performance, and broken his leg. In America he made his first appearance on the stage after an absence of many weeks. It is probable that his leg still bothered him, for although he had been engaged as *premier danseur,* Mme. Lecomte's brother, Jules Martin, seems to have danced most of the leading roles, while Marius was relegated to pantomimic parts. This broken leg may even explain why Marius never became as fine a classic dancer as his brother Lucien.

The month of October was spent in rehearsals. Just before the company was ready to open, the theatre at which they had contracted to appear was burned down. J. W. Wallack, the manager, hurriedly engaged another house, the National Theatre on Broadway, adjoining Niblo's Gardens.

The first performance took place on October 29, 1839. The ballet was *La Tarentule,* which had been presented at the Paris Opéra on June 24 of the same year, with music by Gasimir Gide and choreography by Jean Coralli. The American program credited Coralli with the story (actually supplied, anonymously, by Scribe), but added: "The Dances arranged and the action of the piece produced under the direction of M. Petitpa (sic), Ballet Director from the principal theatres of Paris, Naples, Vienna, Brussels, etc."[4] Seven months later Fanny Elssler, who had danced the leading role in *La Tarentule* at its Paris première, selected it as the vehicle for her American debut.

In addition to the Petipas, Mme. Lecomte's company included Pauline Desjardins, who later made a name for herself in the United States as DeKorponay's popular partner in the Polka, Klishnig, a German eccentric dancer and mime, and a M. Kaiffer who shared with Marius Petipa and Jules Martin the title of first dancer. In *La Tarentule* it was Martin who danced the principal male role, Luigi. His wife had the important part of Clorinda. One of the Petipas—the program does not distinguish between them—played the pantomimic role of Dr. Omeopatico, a bombastic old creature who served both as villain and butt of the piece's humor.

The review which appeared on November 2 in the *Spirit of the Times* was enthusiastic, and especially noted the fine dancing and acting of Mme. Lecomte and M. Martin, but of the Petipas there was only one tantalizing mention: " . . . The principal newcomers were Mademoiselle Pauline Desjardins, and Messieurs Kaiffer and Petitpa. The lady has a very pretty, pleasing face, and dances with a light, airy step. The gentlemen we will not pretend to judge upon first sight. . ." Which is not very helpful to one who would like to know how Marius Petipa danced at twenty-one!

La Tarentule was repeated twice, sharing the bill on October 31 with Charles Kean's first performance of *Richard III.* On November 4 Jean Petipa presented *Jocko, the Brazilian Ape,* which he had given so many times in Brussels. Klishnig danced the title role, with such success that he later toured the United States as star of his own productions. Petipa took the part of Pedro. The ballet ran for six performances, as afterpiece to Edwin Forrest's interpretations of *Metamora* and *The Gladiator.*

In spite of the combined attractions of ballet and drama, Wallack was losing money. On the twelfth of November the dancers were withdrawn, and by the eighteenth he decided to close the theatre, after having lost $5,000. Probably the Petipas would have been glad to return to Europe at once, had not Lecomte promptly found another engagement at the Bowery Theatre. *Jocko* re-opened there on November 21, with the name of Petipa prominent in the advertisements.

Two days later Jean Petipa produced his third ballet, *Marco Bomba, or the Bragging Sergeant,* with Marius Petipa in the role of Nunez. This ballet had been given for the first time at the Théâtre de la Renaissance, in Paris, on August 23, 1839, a few days before the Petipas sailed for America. The choreographer was M. Ragaine, who had been *premier danseur* at Brussels under Jean Petipa. It is probable that M. Lecomte and the Petipas saw this production before their departure.

The story of *Marco Bomba,* laid in Galicia, concerns the unsuccessful (and not too serious) attempts of a group of village lads to escape conscription into the army. After his return to Brussels in 1843 Jean produced this ballet with considerable success, and much later, in 1878, it appeared in the repertoire of the Imperial Theatre in St. Petersburg, when Marius was at the height of his career as virtual dictator of the Russian ballet.

At the Bowery, however, it was given only three times. This engagement also proved a financial failure. On November 23 the company made a gallant effort to close the season with a flourish, presenting on that evening, for the benefit of Mme. Lecomte, both *Marco Bomba* and a very special "Grand Carnival and Masked Ball, arranged and produced by Monsieur Petipa."

By this time Jean and Marius Petipa, accustomed to State-endowed theatres, were thoroughly disgusted with the lack of success which had attended their efforts. According to L. I. Leshkov, the Soviet biographer of Marius Petipa, M. Lecomte did not pay what he had promised. At any rate, they took the first opportunity to board a sailing vessel bound for France. Neither ever returned to America.

The Lecomte troupe, incidentally, did not disband when its ballet master and *premier danseur* deserted it. During the winter of 1839-40 the company travelled to the Western wilds of Mobile, New Orleans, and St. Louis, and, oddly enough, won triumphant successes (in Jean Petipa's ballets) wherever they appeared. Later Jules Martin danced for a time as the partner of Fanny Elssler, during her American tour. Both Mme.

Lecomte and her brother became permanent residents of the United States, and finally settled down to teach dancing in Philadelphia.

On his return to Europe, Marius Petipa went to Bordeaux as *premier danseur*. There he created four ballets, *La Jolie Bordelaise, L'Intrigue Amoureuse, La Vendage, La Langage des Fleurs*. After dancing and producing in Spain for four years, as the partner of Madame Guy-Stephan, he joined his father in St. Petersburg in 1847. He remained in the service of the Russian Imperial Theatres for fifty-eight years, a living link between the early Romantic ballet and the Diaghilev Ballet which first appeared in Paris in 1909. Marius lived to see the European triumphs of the Russian school he had developed through so many years. He died in St. Petersburg in 1910.

On his return from the United States Jean went back to his former post as ballet master at the Monnaie. His rival Bartholomin was gone, and his reign was undisputed. In Brussels Petipa continued to produce the most popular ballets in the repertoire of the Paris Opéra, shortly after their Paris premières. During the season of 1841-42, he mounted Coralli's master-pieces, *La Tarentule* and *Giselle*.

Petipa remained in Brussels for three more years. In 1843 he invited Fanny Elssler to give a series of guest performances in Brussels. She made her debut on May 31, and during the next month danced all her most popular roles: *La Tarentule, La Sylphide; Nathalie, ou la Laitière Suisse; Giselle,* and *Le Dieu et la Bayadère*. She gave one performance for the benefit of the blind and incurable of Brussels, and another for the benefit of the local corps de ballet.

During the following season Jean Petipa produced no less than four-teen ballets! The climax of an exciting year came in April, when Fanny Cerrito appeared as a guest for a fortnight. She danced *La Sylphide, L'Elève d'Amour, La Somnambule, La Gitana, Giselle,* and a divertisse-ment, *La Lithuanienne*.

The year 1844 concluded Jean Petipa's reign in Brussels, for shortly afterwards he accepted a post as professor at the Imperial Academy of Dancing in St. Petersburg. He taught in Russia for years, but with the exception of *Paquita* and *Le Diable Amoureux*, which he staged for Andreyanova in Moscow in 1847, he actually produced no ballets there. In his classes at the Imperial School he developed many fine Russian dancers, whose talents Marius utilized with such success some years later. Jean Petipa died in St. Petersburg in 1855, at the age of sixty-eight.

II

Lucien, eldest son of Jean Petipa, was at one time even more famous than his brother Marius. For many years he was *premier danseur* and ballet master of the Paris Opéra. Although he was a better dancer, he lacked the creative faculty which distinguished the work of his brother. Today, he is almost forgotten because he appeared at a time when the ballerina was all-important, and male dancers were given little opportunity to distinguish themselves.

Born in Marseilles in 1815, Lucien spent his childhood with his parents in Brussels. After several years in the provincial theatres of France, he made his debut at the Paris Opéra on June 10, 1839, in the role of James in *La Sylphide.* His partner was the lovely Dane, Lucile Grahn. Petipa's success was immediate, and he won a secure and permanent place for himself at the Opéra. Théophile Gautier, the poet who wrote the book for *Giselle,* declared that there were only two male dancers at the Opéra worth watching, Lucien Petipa and Auguste Mabille.

Charles Hervey's *The Theatres of Paris,* published in 1844, said of Lucien: " . . . He is remarkably active, and dances with more ease and grace than any of his comrades. . ." It was further noted that he was unusually handsome, although he sometimes compromised his good looks by baring his teeth in a forced grin while he was dancing. Later he conquered this mannerism, and became a fine mime.

It was Lucien who created the role of Albrecht in *Giselle.* After the first performance, June 28, 1841, Gautier wrote: "Petipa was gracious, passionate, and touching. It is a long time since a *danseur* has given so much pleasure or been so well received."[5] "Petipa also merits great eulogies," commented another critic. "He is a *danseur* whom one can watch without laughing, for he never expresses in his person the desire to be admired."[6]

Later in 1841 Lucien won new praise for a *pas de trois* danced with Adèle and Sophie Dumilâtre in *La Reine de Chypre.* His success in *Giselle,* however, caused him to be selected as permanent partner for Carlotta Grisi, and henceforth he danced in each new ballet created for her at the Opéra. They also studied together daily in the class of M. Barrez, a veteran who had been at the Paris Opéra for twenty years. The lovely Carlotta was at that time living with Jules Perrot, a magnificent dancer who had the misfortune of being extremely ugly. Théophile Gautier loved her with a deep and hopeless passion which endured throughout his lifetime. It was to Lucien Petipa, however, that Grisi gave her heart. The handsome dancer appealed to her more than any of the wealthy and distinguished suitors who besieged her. At one time it was whispered that Lucien and Carlotta were married, but the rumor proved false.

In *La Péri,* Carlotta Grisi was obliged to execute a dangerous and difficult leap, in which she fell from a high piece of scenery into the waiting arms of her partner. Only to Petipa, who danced Achmet, would she trust her life in the execution of this breath-taking tour de force. He accompanied her to London when she danced *La Péri* at Drury Lane. Later, he danced with her at the Paris Opéra in *Le Diable à Quatre, Paquita, Griseldis,* and *La Filleule des Fées.*

As *premier danseur* at the Opéra, he was cast for a leading role in almost every ballet presented there. In 1844 he appeared as Télémaque in *Eucharis.* Adèle Dumilâtre danced the title role. Petipa danced *La Péri* with Adeline Plunkett on the occasion of her debut, March 31, 1845. Later he was the partner of Fanny Cerrito in *Orfa and Gemma.* At almost every appearance the press heralded him as the finest male dancer at the Opéra, but these eulogies manage to say very little about his actual style. He must have been a brilliant technician; it is certain that he was a deft and self-effacing partner, a clever mime, and a sincere artist.

"Besides Mlle. Priora, who plays the role of Blanche, and Mlle. Plunkett, who plays that of Vert-Vert," wrote Paul Smith after the première of *Vert-Vert,* "it is necessary to mention Petipa, who plays no role at all, but who dances a *pas de deux* with Mlle. Priora, and supports her very easily in the most difficult evolutions, like a man accustomed to render such services. If great *danseuses* are rare, how much more are great *danseurs!"*[7]

He danced again with Priora in the première of the Mazilier-Potier-Cambon ballet, *Aelia et Mysis,* in 1853. In this tragic ballet Madame Guy-Stephan, the partner of Marius Petipa during his travels in Spain, appeared at the Paris Opéra.

Lucien's fame was not confined to Paris. He had danced, as we have already noted, in London. In 1844 he appeared as guest artist at the Monnaie. There he performed *Giselle, La Péri,* and *La Sylphide.* In 1845 he toured England, Ireland, and Scotland as the partner of Marie Taglioni. The great ballerina presented him with a magnificent diamond brooch, in testimony of her admiration for his performance in the ballet *La Fille de Marbre.* On December 26, 1849, he made his debut at La Scala, Milan, in Casati's ballet *Giovanni di Leida.* Casati was a composer as well as a choreographer, and often assisted in the preparation of the music for his ballets. On this occasion his collaborator was C. B. Croff. *Giovanni di Leida* had considerable success, and Lucien remained in Milan throughout the winter season.

When Carolina Rosati made her Paris Opéra debut in *Jovita,* in 1853, Petipa played his first character role, that of a brigand chieftain. A similar part in the ballet *La Fonti* followed. Petipa had now attained the age of thirty-nine, and although he had not retired from the stage, he decided to turn his attention to choreography. His first effort was a divertissement for the Paris première of Verdi's opera *Les Vêspres Siciliennes,* presented June 13, 1855. "Let us not forget the divertissement of the *Four Seasons,* of which the composition, the tableaux, and the dances do honor to the inventive mind of Petipa . . ." wrote a critic in reviewing the opera.[8]

When Amalia Ferraris danced *Les Elfes,* it was noted that Petipa, "the most distinguished of the princes and dukes of the Opéra,"[9] was Duke Albert.

In 1857 he composed a Spanish dance, *La Gaditana,* which was interpolated in Donizetti's opera *La Favorite.* The following year he attempted his first full-length ballet, *Sacountala,* with a libretto by Gautier and music by Ernest Reyer. The principal role was danced by Ferraris, and Petipa himself appeared as Douchmata, King of India. "Petipa plays his role as king and choreographer with much dignity,"[10] was the only comment vouchsafed by the critic of *La Revue et Gazette Musicale de Paris* after the first performance. Petipa's choreography was probably clean-cut and workmanlike without being either brilliant or particularly original.

The great ballerina Marie Taglioni had retired from the stage in 1847. In 1859, however, she danced with Lucien Petipa at a private performance given at the home of the composer Rossini. His soirées with their attendant buffets were famous, and invitations were much sought after in the musical and artistic circles of Paris. Sometimes Rossini himself would play the piano, or accompany the singer of the day in an aria from one of his operas. Adelina Patti was a frequent guest. On this occasion the two dancers presented a little ballet composed of a gavotte and the famous Tyrolienne from *William Tell.* Taglioni was fifty-five and Petipa forty-three.

Taglioni had been drawn back to Paris by the sensational debut of Emma Livry, who became her pupil. The promising young dancer's career was tragically cut short when she caught fire and suffered severe burns during a rehearsal. She died a few months later, in the summer of 1863, and the sad task of delivering the funeral oration fell to Lucien Petipa.

In 1860 Petipa was appointed professor of the class of perfection at the Opéra, replacing M. Gosselin, who had recently died. He composed his second ballet, *Graziosa,* in the following year. The music was written by Théodore Labarre, the decors were by Cambon and Thierry, and the leading role was danced by Amalia Ferraris. The first performance took place on March 25, 1861.

Rehearsals for this ballet were interrupted by an assignment as difficult as it was unwelcome. On Lucien Petipa devolved the task of arranging the choreography of the Venusberg Bacchanale for the first Paris production of Richard Wagner's *Tannhäuser*, already produced in Dresden in 1845.

The original version contained no ballet, but when Alphonse Royer, director of the Paris Opéra, accepted *Tannhäuser* for production fifteen years later, he demanded that a ballet divertissement be inserted, according to the convention of the time, in the second act. Wagner refused point-blank, as the scene in the Hall of Song contained no appropriate place for a ballet. Royer pointed out that the most influential subscribers of the Opéra, and especially the members of the notorious Jockey Club, came to the Opéra chiefly to see the ballet, and since they always arrived late and left early, the ballet must be in the second act or as a compromise there must be a ballet divertissement between acts one and two. The dispute was quite public and arguments for and against the *Tannhäuser* ballet appeared in the daily papers. At one time Wagner even threatened to withdraw his opera, rather than submit to a change which he felt was a violation of artistic truth. Later, in his treatise *On Conducting,* he took great pains to explain his attitude, emphasizing the fact that he objected not to dancing itself (he included a ballet in *Rienzi*), but to the introduction of a superfluous divertissement which would serve no purpose in the development of the opera. He wrote:

> I had declared that I could not possibly disturb the course of just this second act by a ballet, which must here be senseless from every point of view; while on the other hand I thought the first act, at the voluptuous court of Venus, would afford the most apposite occasion for a choreographic scene of amplest meaning, *since I myself had not deemed possible to dispense with dance in my first arrangement of that scene* (italics the author's). Indeed I was quite charmed with the idea of strengthening an undoubtedly weak point in my earlier score, and I drafted an exhaustive plan for raising this scene in the Venusberg to one of great importance. . . Thus I myself was taken with a new liking for this earlier work of mine: I most carefully revised the score afresh, entirely rewrote the scene of Venus and the ballet-scene preceding it, and everywhere sought to bring the vocal parts into closest agreement with the translated text . . .[11]

Although the first performance of *Tannhäuser* was tentatively scheduled for the last week in January, 1861, Wagner continued to put off the composition of the Bacchanale, and on December 15, 1860, it had not even been begun! The première was finally postponed until March 13, but even so Petipa must have had very little time to prepare a ballet such as Wagner had visualized.[12] At the same time, the choreographer was occupied with preparations for *Graziosa*, which he probably considered much more important than Wagner's first-act Bacchanale! At any rate, Petipa's choreography came far from satisfying Wagner, who wrote later:

I explained to the ballet master what a ludicrous contrast the wretched little tripping *pas* of his Maenads and Bacchantes presented with my music, and begged him to devise something answering to the Bacchanalian groups on famous reliefs, something bold and sublime. The man whistled through his fingers, and said: "Oh, I quite understand, but it would need a corps of *premières danseuses*. Were I to tell my people a word of it, and ask them to strike the attitudes you mean, we should have the Can-can on the spot, and all be ruined. . ."[13]

Petipa's allusion to the *can-can* demonstrated that he knew the popular dance halls and theatres of the Boulevards, although he seldom if ever used contemporary social dances as material for his choreography. The placing of the ballet in the first act precluded the use of outstanding soloists, as they refused to appear if their audience was not there.

The Paris *Tannhäuser* was a complete fiasco, and was withdrawn after three performances. The critics, prejudiced in advance, condemned it unanimously. P. J. Scudo, writing in the influential *Revue des Deux Mondes,* went as far as to say:

It is high time that the Parisian public arrested with one vigorous blow the pretentions of the author of *Tannhäuser.* Without ever having doubted the inanity of his efforts to change the tastes and the good sense of France, we hope that M. Wagner, his system and his work will be promptly judged and forgotten . . .[14]

Since this was typical of the attitude of the time towards Wagner, one can hardly condemn Lucien Petipa for having failed to translate his music adequately into dance form.

The success of *Graziosa* helped Petipa to forget his part in the Wagnerian disaster, and a few weeks later he welcomed his brother Marius, who had just arrived with his wife on a visit from Russia. Lucien arranged for Marius's ballet *Le Marché des Innocents* to be presented at the Opéra in May, and for this production Lucien assisted in the staging. In October of this eventful year, Lucien composed the dances for a revival of Gluck's *Alceste.*

The next work which he created was *Le Roi d'Yvetot,* presented December 28, 1865. A serious illness interrupted his work in 1868, and he was obliged to retire for some time. During the season of 1872-73 he directed the ballet and the school of dancing at the Monnaie, but he presented no ballets of his own. The two productions of the year were his brother's *Le Marché des Innocents* and a ballet by Lagye, with music by Hanssens, called *Les Fleurs Animées* (which seems to stem from Grand-ville's drawings and Didelot's *Flore et Zéphyr*).

Lucien Petipa's last choreographic composition was Edouard Lalo's *Namouna*. It was presented at the Paris Opéra on March 6, 1882, with Rita Sangalli in the title role. Because of the "symphonic" character of the music it was not appreciated at its first performance. There were not enough set numbers to display the virtuosity of the soloists. Perhaps Lalo and Petipa had unconsciously adopted ideas crystalized in Wagner's music. When the ballet was revived in 1908 with new choreography by Léo Staats, the score was hailed as a masterpiece.

Lucien Petipa died in 1900, forgotten by all save a few of his associates. His fame had rested upon his own splendid abilities as a dancer, rather than on his achievements as a choreographer. He had upheld the honor of the male dancer in an age when he was the most neglected of artists; for this alone he may be remembered.

III

Some thirty years ago, the Diaghilev Russian Ballet appeared in Paris for the first time, and made history. It is not so well remembered, however, that individual Russian dancers had been appearing in Paris at intervals throughout the nineteenth century. Marius Petipa went there himself in 1861, for the debut of his wife, the young and lovely Marie Petipa, at the Opéra.

Through the influence of his brother Lucien, Marius arranged for *Le Marché des Innocents* to be presented in the French capital. He had created the work in St. Petersburg, to Pugni's score, where it was first given on April 23, 1859. The Paris première took place on May 29, two years later.

Although the new ballet was a decided success, the French criticisms devoted but little space to discussion of its choreography. Their attention was centered upon the charming prima ballerina, Marie Sergeyevna Surovschikova, professionally known by her married name as Marie Petipa.

Petipa was one of the first Russian ballerinas to venture outside her native country. In Paris she had been preceded by Nadezhda Bog-danova, who had danced there from 1851 to 1855, and by Elena Andreyanova, who had appeared there in 1845. Marie Petipa, thanks to the careful tutelage of her husband, was able to surpass both of her predecessors and increase the prestige of the Russian ballet in Europe.

Marie Petipa was a fragile girl with delicate limbs and flexible, arrowlike pointes. Her figure differed greatly from that of the typical sturdy ballerina of the 'sixties. She was not strong enough to execute tours de force of great difficulty and brilliancy, but she had an instinctive flair for character dancing. In *Le Marché des Innocents* she danced an exotic solo called *La Ziganka*, as well as a Mazurka and a classic *pas de deux* with Mérante, called *Le Panier des Cerises*. At the first performance she was recalled after each of these dances, while the audience shouted and clapped its approval.

"Mme. Marie Petipa, although still quite young, is not making her first debut," wrote the critic of *La Revue et Gazette Musicale de Paris*. "She has already gathered many bravos and crowns. She is slim of figure, with a slender body, alluringly svelte, a delicate leg, and she has *pointes* which she uses like little natural stilts, with an invariable and formidable precision. One would say (all play on words aside) that they are *pointes* of steel! The audience found her charming, and applauded her rapturously in the *Panier des Cerises*, a *pas* which she danced with Mérante and which ended with a graceful imitation of the prayer of Tantalus. It is necessary to see the supple ballerina bend and lower herself in trying to seize with an eager mouth the fruit which is on the ground and which always escapes her. . ."[15]

On July 12, 1861, she danced her role of Gloriette in *Le Marché des Innocents* on an historic occasion. It was the first time that a whole evening devoted to ballet was presented at the Paris Opéra. The rest of the program consisted of *La Vivandière*, danced by Mlle. Zina Richard, who was also a Russian, and Lucien Petipa's ballet *Graziosa*, danced by Mlle. Amalia Ferraris.

At the command performance of *Le Marché des Innocents* for the Emperor of the French and the King of Sweden, the latter visited the *Foyer de la Danse* to congratulate the charming Russian ballerina. On the following evening a performance was given for her benefit. It was completely sold out in advance, and the receipts exceeded 16,000 francs. M. de Sabouroff, director of the Russian Imperial Theatres, was present, as well as the Princess Metternich, the French Minister of State, and numerous members of the Russian aristocracy. On this occasion Marie Petipa danced a new divertissement called *Pas Cosmopolitana*, which had been arranged by Jules Perrot in Russia. Unfortunately its presentation in Paris had not been authorized by the choreographer, who promptly sued Marius Petipa for appropriating his composition. After a lawsuit which dragged on for nearly a year, Petipa was forced to pay Perrot 300 francs damages.

When Marius and Marie Petipa returned to Russia it was with greatly increased prestige. Glowing accounts of their Parisian triumphs preceded them to St. Petersburg. Their position in Russia was infinitely strengthened by their foreign conquests. It was during the following winter at the Maryinsky that Marius Petipa composed his first five-act ballet, *La Fille du Pharaon* (music by Pugni), which enjoyed a stunning success.

Marie Petipa returned to Paris in March, 1862. She made her reappearance on June 6 in *Le Marché des Innocents*, and was welcomed with the following enthusiastic notice: "Mme. Petipa has something in her which radiates joy and contentment, and communicates itself magnetically to the public. . . She is so happy to dance, she seems at the same time so penetrated by the pleasure which she causes, that one feels this influence immediately, and gives oneself up to it with infinite pleasure. . ."[16]

On June 20 *Le Diable à Quatre*, which had been created for Carlotta Grisi in 1845, was revived for Marie Petipa. It was the occasion of the following eulogy:

. . . The talent of Mme. Petipa is a talent all her own; one cannot make any comparison between her and the stars of the past or present. . . . She dances with her legs, with her arms, with her fingers, with her head; she leaps, she pirouettes, she waltzes on the *pointes* (and what *pointes*) for fully five minutes, and all this with a lightness, an aplomb, a happiness, a coquettishness, which charm, which seduce, which conquer. For two hours, such was the effect produced upon the public by Mme. Petipa, an effect which was translated into applause and bravos without end, and frequent recalls. But it was above all in the Mazurka that she exercized all her native seductions; we do not believe that this dance, so graceful and so original, has ever been danced in this manner in Paris. The partner of Mme. Petipa, Kchesinsky, dances like a child of Poland and proved himself accomplished; also the public called encore loudly, and even recalled the couple, who graciously began to dance again. Already, in *Le Marché des Innocents*, Mme. Petipa had given proof of the intelligence and spirit with which she mimes a role; one has been convinced by the scene of the mirror and by the dancing lesson that in this respect she has nothing to learn. It would be impossible to express better her new situation as a great lady, or more comically her impatience at the dancing lessons . . .[17]

The Kchesinsky mentioned in the review, who had accompanied Marie Petipa to Paris for the express purpose of dancing the Mazurka with her, was the father of the great Imperial ballerina Mathilda Kchesinskaia, friend of the last Czar, now wife of the Grand Duke. From her balcony V. I. Lenin announced the formation of the Soviet State.

Marie Petipa remained at the Paris Opéra for the whole summer. On one occasion Kchesinsky was ill, and not wishing to omit the famous Mazurka she danced it alone, improvising some movements with great cleverness and ingenuity. Later she took part in a pension fund performance, appearing in *Le Diable à Quatre* and the divertissement from Halévy's *La Juive*.

In the autumn, after paying a flying visit to London and another to Germany, the family returned to St. Petersburg. There Marie made a triumphant reappearance in her husband's *La Fille du Pharaon*. Her magnificent work as the interpreter of his early ballets helped Marius Petipa enormously in establishing himself as the principal choreographer of the Russian school. After the withdrawal of Saint-Léon, in 1869, he was appointed chief *maître de ballet*. In that capacity he arranged *Raymonda*, *La Belle au Bois Dormant*, *Le Lac des Cygnes* and those other masterpieces that we still enjoy.

The health of Marie Petipa was too delicate to long withstand the strain of dancing. She retired from the stage in 1869, and died in Pyatigorsk, Northern Caucasia, in March, 1882. Meanwhile, on January 12, 1875, at the Maryinsky, beautiful eighteen-year-old Marie Mariusovna had made her debut in *The Blue Dahlia*, composed for her mother fifteen years before.

—Dance Index; Vol I, No. 5, May 1942.

[1] This picture is ten feet and a quarter by eight and three quarters.

[2] Deshayes and Perrot staged *Giselle* in London in 1842.

[3] Some years later Bartholomin visited the United States as ballet master and mime of the Monplaisir Ballet Company, which made its first appearance at the Broadway Theatre, New York, on October 21, 1847, in *L'Almee*. Bartholomin remained in America for a year, directing the Monplaisir productions of *La Jenne Dalmate*, *La Folie d'un Peintre*, *Les Deux Roses*, *Azelia*, and *Le Diable à Quatre*.

[4] If Jean Petipa produced ballets in Paris, it must have been at one of the minor theatres. He was never choreographer at the Paris Opéra or at any of the other important theatres of which we have record. During the periods when his long service at the Monnaie was interrupted, however (1831-33 and 1835-39), we have record of his work in Lyon, Marseilles and Bordeaux.

[5] *Historie de l'Art Dramatique en France*, Vol. I, p. 42.

[6] *La Revue et Gazette Musicale de Paris*, July 4, 1841.

[7] *La Revue et Gazette Musicale de Paris*, 1851, p. 388.

[8] Ibid., 1853, p. 186.

[9] Ibid., 1856, p. 262.

[10] Ibid., 1858, p. 238.

[11] Richard Wagner: *Prose Works*, translated by William Ashton Ellis. Volume III, pp. 351-362.

[12] Wagner's directions for the Venusberg scene are as follows: The stage represents the interior of the hill of Venus. In the furthest background, there is a bluish lake in which

maidens are bathing, and on whose banks Sirens are reclining. Venus is extended on a couch in the left foreground. Tannhäuser's face is buried in her knees. The cave has a rosy hue. From the mounds on the side of the cave where tender couples are reclining come the nymphs who dance. . . A group of bacchantes dash thru the nymphs and stir them to frantic excitement. They are joined by Satyrs and faunes. The Graces and the cupids now take part in the orgy. . . At the height of the dance, a sudden lassitude spreads and a mist gathers in the cave leaving only Tannhäuser and Venus visible.

[13] Richard Wagner: *Prose Works,* translated by William Ashton Ellis. Volume IV, pp. 342-343.

[14] *Revue des Deux Mondes,* April 1, 1861, p. 769.

[15] *La Revue et Gazette Musicale de Paris,* 1861, p. 169.

[16] *La Revue et Gazette Musicale de Paris,* 1862, p. 189.

[17] *La Revue et Gazette Musicale de Paris,* 1862, p. 201.

A German caricature of Fanny Elssler straddling the Atlantic Ocean,
holding a bag marked "Thaler" in her left hand and one marked
"Dollars" in her right. (Collection of Louis Péres)

XI: New York in the Forties as Seen by Fanny Elssler

THE SECOND QUARTER of the nineteenth century has long been known as the golden age of the ballet. During this period there flourished the exquisite Carlotta Grisi, dainty Fanny Cerrito, the great Taglioni, and that beautiful, sparkling, unique artist, "the divine" Fanny Elssler.

After long and ardent study in her native city of Vienna, where her father was copyist to Haydn, Fanny Elssler succeeded, at an extremely early age, in bringing the theatregoers of London, Berlin and Naples to her twinkling feet. A few months later she had conquered the artistic centre of Europe, Paris. Looking about for new worlds to conquer she decided to visit America.

At that time the United States was considered by many to be a wilderness entirely unfit to appreciate such a delicate art as that of the ballet. Nevertheless, the fearless Fanny took her artistic life in her hands and set out. About two years later a New York firm published a quaint little volume containing the *Letters and Journal of Fanny Elssler*. From these letters a complete idea of her struggles, disappointments and triumphs can be obtained. [These letters were in fact written by Fanny Elssler's manager Henry Wikoff, but must have been founded on his conversations with the ballerina.—I. G.]

A letter to one of her dearest friends contains a fascinating account of her early struggles, as well as a sincere tribute to her ballet master, the former idol of Europe, Auguste Vestris:

Paris, January, 1840
. . . I never worked harder than I have this winter, and that chiefly to soothe the anxiety of dear old professor Vestris. You have heard me seldom speak of this interesting person, whose professional reputation formerly filled Europe. The once brilliant *dieu de la danse* has dwindled, as we all must, into wrinkled and decrepit age, and his only delight now, he declares, is to play the fiddle as I practice daily

before him. This is his only occupation, and he declares he lives his past life over again in me. I confess, with gratitude, my indebtedness to his genius, taste and vigilant attention.

When I came to Paris, I thought I had reached the topmost round of my art. I had already exhausted every known difficulty and invented new, but I saw Taglioni and grew alarmed. I felt the ordeal through which I had to pass would be final and might be fatal, for the standard of *la danse* I found so much higher in France.

Fortunately for me, Signor Vestris became interested in me, and endeavored to raise me up to his own lofty ideas of the art. For three months I toiled as a galley slave before I would *consent* to appear. The very expectation that prevailed frightened me to greater efforts, and the enormous strides I made in advance taught me that in the dance, at least, one's education is never finished. It was not so much in elementary studies that I gained from Vestris, but rather in style and tone. He sought to give me grace and expression—in short, his *finish* to my poses and carriage—and the triumphant success of my debut, he said, repaid him a thousand times. I shall never forget his despair when, after my sad illness of 1836, he found that I had certainly *lost my art*. You recollect my prostration was so complete I had to be taught to walk again; but when I essayed to dance I found to my horror that I was utterly incapable of executing the commonest feats of the *foyer*. With desperation in every limb, I sought, day after day, to recover my lost facility. Vestris soothed me and encouraged me by turns, till he groaned and wept over the dreadful apprehension that all was lost. This went on for weeks, when one memorable day I felt a sudden and magical return of my force, and with a cry of delight I bounded into the air, and danced till I fell breathless on the floor.

Another letter describes Fanny Elssler's position in Paris at the height of her career:

Paris, November, 1839

Have I not all that a reasonable woman, if there is such a being to be found, could desire? My professional career has reached its zenith; here I am, sitting securely on an operatic throne that has dazzled my eye and fired my ambition since my girlhood. *Le grand Monarque* never swayed more completely over the wills of his admiring subjects than I do over the rapt fancies of my enthusiastic admirers of the *Opéra*. Never was *artiste* more completely seated in public sympathy, undisturbed by rivalry, unassailed by critics, and popular even with that formidable foe, the claque. The curtain is drawn, and I appear, to be welcomed with smiles that make the theatre glow " 'neath their sunny warmth"; I dance, and rapturous applause cheers me to loftiest efforts; I curtsy, and flowers and garlands cover me. And then the delights, more intoxicating still, of the *entr'acte*. I quit the scene for my boudoir, whose silken splendor owes all its elegance to the taste and liberality of my kind *directeur*. What do you see, Mina, in its sparkling mirrors? What a gay, gallant, and graceful throng encircle me, occupying every chair, besieging every sofa! And have I not reason to be proud of homage from such a *levée*, representing the rank, the wit, the elegance, of this brilliant capital—the white-gloved denizens of the *avant-scènes*, whose "bravo" is the fiat of our scenic fate?

During this period there was an intense rivalry between Taglioni, the ethereal goddess of the dance, and Elssler, the fiery, voluptuous creature of earth. It is, therefore, immensely interesting to learn Elssler's opinion of her rival:

> Paris, February, 1840.
>
> . . . Taglioni was then at the very height of her renown; the matchless creation, *La Sylphide*, had carried her reputation to the uttermost ends of Europe, and her nightly performances at the *Opéra* were hailed with enthusiastic plaudits by her enraptured admirers, and truly her execution was superb and faultless. Graceful as a swan, she glided majestically across the scene, leaving in her wake mute wonder and delight. No one comprehended her perfection more fully, no one enjoyed it more heartily, than I did. Is it wonderful, then, that I trembled when I stepped forth, night after night, to contest with her the coveted palm of superiority, and divide with her the spoils of public favor? This rivalry, I dare say painful to both, was kept on for a year or two, when she left the *Opéra* for Russia, where her success only equalled her great merits.

It was in 1839 that Elssler made her momentous decision to visit the wilderness of America. Her admirers felt that she was throwing away what promised to be a sensational European career, yet she persevered in her intention, and won an overwhelming success in this country, where it is said that Congressmen pulled her carriage through the streets to her hotel after a performance in Washington. The dancer's first hesitation at visiting the strange new land is explained by the following remarkable letter:

> Paris, December, 1839.
> Dear Mina,
>
> . . . I dare say, with your usual activity in such matters, you have been buying a map with America drawn on it, and its cities, its mountains, and towns, for I suppose it has got its share of those necessities that most countries stand in need of. Do tell me something about it. I don't believe my stupid old schoolmaster ever heard of it, for he never told me anything of it that I recollect. I know a great deal more of the moon; at least I have seen *that*. When shall I behold this unknown part of our planet? I ought to be ashamed of my ignorance, no doubt, but I see wiser people about me who never wish to know of any place out of Paris—the world's epitome. There are some complacent Parisians who doubt the existence of Germany at all, or at the most, admit that there *may* be such *barbarians*. Every day I hear some acquaintance ask of America, "Qu'est que c'est que cela?"

Needless to say, Elssler found New York to be scarcely as barbarous as she had anticipated. Her description of the harbor would never be recognized as such in this day of skyscrapers and steamers, yet the sight of the "numberless villas along the seacoast," and the "lovely promenade called the Battery" seem to have made an extraordinarily favorable impression on the little Austrian *danseuse.*

May 3, 1840.

. . . Look there, Mina, behold America! Since daylight we have seen land, and since that, how have I been staring, till my sight has grown dim and confused. We have passed the Hook, a point of land around which we turned into a fine stream between two islands looking almost like a canal, leading straight to the harbor of New York. As we go steaming rapidly along in smooth water, I am every moment enchanted by the lively landscapes that present themselves, so entirely unlike anything I ever saw or fancied. Hill and dale decked in the highest verdure and luxuriating in the richest foliage, succeed in the most pleasing variety. Numberless villas are dotted along the sea-coast, all painted in dazzling white, relieved by green Venetian blinds. These pretty objects are to me so perfectly novel, that I am exclaiming with delight every moment.

The harbor of New York opens upon us. Can anything in nature be more magnificent? Islands of the most picturesque beauty are scattered in every direction the eye wanders to. The city itself is an object of wonderful attraction. A lovely promenade called the Battery, adorned with splendid trees and pretty walks, and running from the water's edge, may be considered its natural frontispiece, and nothing can be more strikingly beautiful to the eyes of a stranger.

During the two weeks' voyage she had been unable to practice her dancing, and feared that such long neglect of her art might lessen her powers. However, she soon found that this was not the case. On May 9, 1840, just one week after her arrival, her New York debut took place. Her account reads like a page from some thrilling novel:

May 16, 1840.

I am satisfied, nay, far more, rejoiced to my inmost heart, by the unexpected manifestations of popular feelings in my favor; but I will relate to you the history of the night. I was nervous beyond anything I ever experienced before; this was natural, and I have partly explained it already. I trembled in every limb with apprehensions I could not control; I had hardly strength to walk upon the stage. The curtain rose, and breathless silence prevailed; the music struck up, and the moment came, and I appeared. The scene that ensued beggars description. The *whole house* rose, and such a shout ascended as stunned my senses, and made me involuntarily recoil. Men waved their hats, and women their handkerchiefs, and all was inexplicable dumb show for several mortal moments. I stood confounded, and tears streamed down my face. Order at length restored, the dance began. I danced without effort, and even Katty applauded some of my feats. The most deafening exclamations of delight broke at rapid internals from all parts of the house, till they lashed themselves into a perfect tempest of admiration. Never before did I behold so vast an assembly so completely under the sway of *one* dominant feeling, and so entirely abandoned to its inspiration. The curtain fell amid a roar that sounded like the fall of mighty waters, and that soon brought me before them. Their applause was perfectly frantic, cheers and bravos saluted me, and flowers and wreaths fell like rain upon me.

That was the New York debut of Fanny Elssler. By the enthusiastic welcome which they extended to the young continental artist, the American public showed a whole-hearted interest in the art of Terpsichore, which has grown with the passing of years.

"The divine Fanny," after a triumphant tour through the eastern cities, and a visit to Havana, returned to Paris with her fame not lessened, but increased. Her career, until her retirement in 1851, was a series of triumphs rarely equalled in the annals of the theatre.

—*Theatre Guild Magazine*, November 1929.

Fanny Elssler in the Cracovienne from *The Gypsy*. (Collection of
Allison Delarue)

XII: Ballet Slippers and Bunker Hill

AMONG the official documents which repose in state in the cornerstone of Bunker Hill Monument there is—if tradition be correct—one small and dainty pair of pink satin ballet slippers. They were placed there nearly a century ago, as a permanent remembrance of the generosity of one of the grestest dancers the world has ever known, Fanny Elssler.

When, in 1840, "the Divine Fanny" decided to conquer new worlds in the strange and savage wilds of distant America, she already had a long and brilliant career behind her. It had begun in Vienna some twenty years earlier, and continued with increasing success through Italy, Germany, England and France, where her performances at the Paris Opéra made ballet history. Her *Cachucha* was as famous in her time as Pavlova's *Dying Swan* has been in ours. Elssler's decision to visit America was made against the advice of her most trusted friends, and even her beloved elder sister Therese, who was also a dancer, refused to accompany her on this mad excursion. Fanny, however, never had cause to regret her decision.

Her arrival in New York was considered an event of the greatest importance. The *New York Weekly Herald* devoted three of its five front-page columns to the chronicle of her activities. Her appearances at the Park Theatre were sensationally successful, and saved the manager from bankruptcy, while her presence in a box on the evenings when she was not dancing was an attraction sufficient to insure a crowded house. On these latter occasions she was frequently escorted by "Prince" John Van Buren, son of the President of the United States.

When Fanny danced in Washington, the Senate was closed on nights when she appeared, because it would have been impossible to obtain a quorum. After a performance in Baltimore, some fashionable young men-about-town unhitched the horses from her carriage, put themselves in harness, and pulled the flower-laden vehicle through the streets to the doors of her hotel, where they serenaded her until the small hours of the morning. Her arrival in Richmond was heralded by tolling bells and booming cannon.

All this extravagant adulation of "a foreign opera-dancer" caused considerable comment in the press of the nation. Fanny's detractors claimed, rather absurdly, that she was nothing more or less than a beautiful female who made an indecent exhibition of herself on the stage. Her even more vociferous adherents replied that these barbarous Americans who did not admire Elssler were crudely unappreciative of the subtleties of art. Had not Paris and London set the seal of their approval upon Fanny's dancing?

The center of the maelstrom of controversy which raged about Fanny where she went was, strangely enough, conservative Boston. If Fanny had been applauded in other cities, she was idolized in the city on the Charles. She first appeared at the Tremont Theatre on September 7, 1840, in the ballet *La Tarentule* and the brief divertissement *La Cracovienne*. The boxes had been sold at auction, one of them fetching the incredible sum of $24. Fanny stayed in Boston for an entire month, dancing in *Nathalie, La Sylphide, La Rose Annimée*, and various other ballets. Her most popular divertissement was, naturally, the intoxicating Spanish *Cachucha*. Fanny was frequently serenaded, and dignified citizens prowled indiscreetly about the Tremont House, hoping to get a glimpse of the lovely dancer.

During this engagement there occurred an incident which has since become famous. Ralph Waldo Emerson and Margaret Fuller were attending a performance of Elssler's, and both were entranced by the revelation of beauty inherent in the dancer's supreme mastery of her art. "Ralph," said Miss Fuller, "this is poetry." "No, Margaret," he replied, "it is religion."

Elssler was anxious to leave behind her some permanent souvenir of the sincere affection she felt for Boston and its people. Her arrival there had chanced to coincide with the opening of a great bazaar held by the ladies of the city for the benefit of the Bunker Hill Monument Fund. The whole town was agog with excitement over the possibility of the completion of the memorial shaft. Unfortunately, the proceeds of the fair amounted to little over $30,000, while $60,000 was needed to finish the monument. Elssler saw here an excellent opportunity to prove the depth of her gratitude. On September 26, she wrote a most demure and proper letter to Mr. J. T. Buckingham, president of the Bunker Hill Monument Association, offering either the flat sum of $1,000, or her professional services, to be used according to the discretion of the committee.

Mr. Buckingham promptly accepted her offer, and it was decided that a benefit performance should be held at the Tremont Theatre on October 1. The event went off well; the theatre was crowded with the elite of New England aristocracy; Fanny danced *La Sylphide*, the *Cachucha*, and the *Cracovienne*, and made a charming little speech in her imperfect German-English concerning the "two monuments that would henceforth rise together—one of granite, on Bunker's Hill, the other, of gratitude, in my heart." About $1,100 was turned over to the committee.

After it was all over, however, it occurred to someone that perhaps it wasn't quite the thing to accept money for a national monument from a foreign dancer. Letters of protest were written to the papers, and as promptly answered by persons who pointed out that Fanny had shown more unselfish generosity than those hypocritical patriots who, while they were loud in their protests against Elssler's gift, had failed to contribute to the fund themselves. Moreover, the objectors were accused of poor taste and lack of chivalry towards a woman and a stranger. The whole affair was discussed, pro and con, in newspapers all over the country. After a long and bitter controversy, the contribution was finally accepted by unanimous vote of the committee in charge. If the slippers which Elssler wore at the benefit performance were actually placed in the cornerstone of the monument, they were smuggled there by some anonymous admirer on the committee.

Fanny, meanwhile, continued her triumphant progress through the United States—a progress which was marked everywhere by a violent disease contemporaneously known as *Fannyelsslermaniaphobia*, which manifested itself in Elssler scarfs, silks and ribbons, Elssler hats, Elssler cuffs, Elssler bootjacks, Elssler jewelry, and even oysters à la *Elssler*. Fanny never forgot Boston, and long after her retirement from the stage she admitted that she held it most dear of all the American cities in which she had danced.

—*American Dancer*, September 1937

A music cover featuring the Monplaisirs during the period of their popularity in America. (Dance Collection, The New York Public Library)

XIII: *Esmeralda* in America

*E*SMERALDA was one of the most opulent theatrical spectacles of the nineteenth century. An example of a long-forgotten facet of the romantic ballet, it was grandiose but realistic. One of the most effective vehicles of the provocative and glamorous Fanny Elssler, it revealed the warm, glowing, earthy side of romanticism. Peopled with beggars, thieves, soldiers and gypsies, it was removed as far as possible from the delicate wood spirits of *La Sylphide* and the haunting willis of *Giselle*.

Jules Perrot, who made *Esmeralda* his choreographic masterpiece, had already conquered his obstacle when he managed to extract a danceable libretto from the rich but ponderous plot of Victor Hugo's famous novel, *Notre Dame de Paris*, best known in English as *The Hunchback of Notre Dame*. Perrot, with his keen sense of the dramatic and his brilliance in handling big ensembles, found stimulation and inspiration in Hugo's panoramic picture of the Paris of the middle ages.

Esmeralda had its première in London in 1844, and was danced in the United States just four years later. Its first American performance took place at the Park Theatre, New York, on September 18, 1848. It was produced by the Monplaisir Ballet, an accomplished troupe of European dancers who had been touring the United States for nearly a year. They had already presented *Le Diable à Quatre, La Folie d'un Peintre*, and other works familiar in the annals of the dance, as well as original ballets by Victor Bartholomin, who had been choreographer at the Théâtre de la Monnaie in Brussels, and by Hippolyte Monplaisir, the leading male dancer.

Esmeralda was the company's greatest success. The American libretto claims that it was patterned faithfully after Perrot's original version, and there is every reason to believe that this is true. Both Monplaisir, who staged it, and his wife Adèle, who danced the title role, had been featured

114

artists at La Scala, Milan, when Perrot himself had produced it there for Fanny Elssler in 1845, the year after the London première.

The plot of *Esmeralda*, even after Perrot's simplifications and adaptions, remains an elaborate and involved affair. It concerns a young gypsy girl who loves Phoebus, a handsome Captain of the Guard, but who marries the penniless poet Pierre Gringoire in order to save him from death at the hands of a band of vagabonds. Things are further complicated by the fact that Phoebus is betrothed to Fleur-de-Lys, while the villainous Claude Frollo, archdeacon of Notre Dame, is infatuated with Esmeralda. Quasimodo, the half-crazed hunchback bell-ringer of Notre Dame, is his accomplice. Frollo attacks Phoebus and then accuses Esmeralda of the murder of her beloved. She is sentenced to die on the scaffold, but is reprieved at the last moment when Phoebus, who was only wounded, reappears and places the blame on Frollo. Somehow the impossible tangle is straightened out and Esmeralda and Phoebus are united.

There are many dramatic details, not touched upon in this scant outline, which must have made *Esmeralda* confusing as well as involved; but the dances were brilliant, the crowd scenes spectacular, and audiences loved it. One of Esmeralda's most effective scenes was her first entrance, where she danced in with a little pet goat.

The roles of Esmeralda, Gringoire, and Phoebus had been created in London by Carlotta Grisi, the original Giselle, Jules Perrot, the choreographer, and Arthur Saint-Léon, virtuoso of the violin as well as a superb ballet technician. In New York they were danced by Adèle and Hippolyte Monplaisir, and a featured member of their company, M. Cornet. Both of the Monplaisirs had been pupils at the private academy of the great teacher Carlo Blasis, in Milan. They had danced in Spain, France and Italy before coming to the United States in 1847. At La Scala, where they had been leading dancers for three seasons (1844-46) they had been closely associated with such celebrated artists as Marie Taglioni, Fanny Elssler, Lucile Grahn and Carolina Rosati, as well as Perrot. At La Scala Hippolyte Monplaisir had danced Albrecht to Fanny Elssler's Giselle.

At the London première of *Esmeralda*, the drawf Quasimodo was played by Coulon (son of the Coulon remembered today as the teacher of Marie Taglioni); in New York the role was danced by an American named Corby, noted chiefly for his comedy roles but equally adept in all sorts of character parts. Fleur-de-Lys was danced in London by Adelaide Frassi, and in New York by Anna Bulan. The original score of Cesare Pugni was used in the American production, but Thomas Hamblin, manager of the Park Theatre, commissioned new costumes and scenery from a whole corps of artists. According to the playbills preserved in the

Harvard Theatre Collection, "Dejonge and Assistants" were responsible for the "Costumes, Properties, Trophies, Banners, etc.," (*Esmeralda* must have been a gala spectacle indeed!), while the decor was the work of "Isherwood, Grain, Porter and assistants."

In the decade before 1848, New York had seen a great deal of first-class ballet. Fanny Elssler had danced there frequently during her two-year sojourn in America; Paul and Amelie Taglioni, Mlle. Celeste, Mme. Augusta, the Paris Opéra ballerina Hermine Blangy, the Italians Giovanna Ciocca and Gaetano Neri, and the Americans Mary Ann Lee and Augusta Maywood were among those who had made classic ballet one of the most popular features of the New York stage. Nevertheless, the Monplaisir *Esmeralda* seems to have created something of a sensation.

"We sincerely confess that, since the days of Fanny Elssler we have never witnessed a triumph equal to that which was awarded last evening to the celebrated Monplaisir troupe," said the *New York Herald* on the morning after the première:

> From the beginning to the end of the ballet of *Esmeralda*, the applause, the enthusiasm were unbounded, and shouts were incessantly drawn from the assembly. Let us say at once that never in the United States has a ballet equal to that produced last night . . . been offered to an American audience. . . . The lovely Esmeralda, as well as the beau Phoebus, the odious priest Frollo, and the horrible monster Quasimodo, are interesting in their parts from beginning to end. . . .: Madame Monplaisir, accompanied by her pretty goat "Djali," deeply impressed the audience and displayed such *jetés battus*, such difficult *sauts*, that she was declared admirable, and worthy of the highest rank as a *danseuse* and a *comedienne*. As for M. Monplaisir, he rendered his part of Gringoire with a *naiveté*, *a bonhomie*, which proved that he deeply knew the character of his part; his dancing was as wonderful as it was difficult. . . .

The scenic investiture came in for its share of praise, as did the other dancers. "M. Cornet gave due credit to his part of Phoebus, and displayed the richest costume we ever saw. As for M. Corby, his Quasimodo was played with skill and truthfulness. Mlle. Anna Bulan, whose pretty figure, and sparkling eyes, have made her a favorite among us, performed her dances with great agility, and received much applause. Great credit is also due to the makers of the gorgeous pagentry and splendid scenery of *Esmeralda*. . . ."

The new ballet was given every night until the middle of October. The English tragedian Macready, who had expected to begin a guest engagement at the Park on the first of the month, was obliged to arrange to appear at another theatre. (The pompous actor hated ballet, so this humiliating experience probably reduced him to a state of helpless fury.)

When *Esmeralda* finally closed, on October 12, the Monplaisir Ballet waited only four days before opening again with *Le Diable à Quatre* and a varied repertoire; but soon *Esmeralda* was back on the bills, and was danced almost nightly throughout November.

In the meantime, the popularity of *Esmeralda* had led to rival productions in several other New York theatres. As early as April, 1848, months before the première of the ballet, the American dancer and actress Julia Turnbull had assumed the title role in a play based on the Hugo novel. In September, at the Bowery Theatre, she acted it again. On October 2 the National Theatre joined the competition by producing a dramatic version of *Esmeralda*, while another was given at the Chatham later that month. Early in November, at the Olympic, the popular American actress and dancer Mary Ann Gannon attempted the part of Esmeralda, in a condensed version of the play, and was damned with faint praise: ". . . She acted very well, sang better, and danced with the greatest possible ease and grace, not to say she quite equalled Mme. Monplaisir . . ." wrote the *Spirit of the Times*.

The Monplaisir *Esmeralda* continued its triumphant career. On December 9 the *Spirit of the Times* commented:

. . . The Monplaisir troupe combine the essentials of a good and effective, although not numerous, corps de ballet, whose pantomime and stage arrangements add to the attractiveness of their dancing, and are consequently enabled to produce pieces belonging to their particular line of art, with a perfection of united taste and tact unknown to other companies. . . .

The Monplaisir Ballet had been booked for a tour of the South, and the New York engagement drew to a close. On December 15, Hippolyte Monplaisir took his benefit performance, dancing to a crowded and enthusiastic house. Adèle's benefit was scheduled for the following evening. Most of the dancers were already in the theatre, putting on their makeup or warming up for the performance, when, a few minutes before six, smoke was seen curling from the prompter's little room at the side of the stage. A file of playbills hanging near a gas jet had blown against the open flame. In a few moments the whole theatre was a blazing inferno. Adèle Monplaisir fainted in her dressing room, and was carried out of the burning building by her maid. All the performers managed to escape before the flames got completely beyond control.

The *New York Evening Post*, on December 18, carried a vivid description of the tragic fire:

. . . At a quarter past six the scene which was presented to the one hundred thousand citizens congregated in the Park, and the one hundred thousand on tops of buildings throughout the city, was one of the grandest conceivable; the flames leaped and frolicked to the height of at least three hundred feet from the ground and giving forth a light which enabled persons at the distance of a mile to read the finest manuscript. The sublimity of the scene was much increased by the darkness of the night. In the space of one short hour the entire building, which had been recently refitted by Mr. Hamblin, with much splendor and at great expense, and the entire contents, saving a small portion of the costumes, was a heap of ruins, the entire loss being not far from $50,000, about half of which falls upon the manager, Mr. Hamblin, who seems the sport of the fates, this being the fourth time that he has been burned out—three times while lessee of the Bowery Theatre. . . .

In spite of this unexpected blow, in which their personal losses must have been enormous, the Monplaisirs managed to pull their company together, and set out on tour. By the following spring they were back in New York enjoying another profitable season, this time at the Broadway Theatre.

Adèle Monplaisir was later to separate from her husband and to tour America with the Ravel troupe of pantomimists and dancers. In 1856, at Niblo's Garden, she danced *Esmeralda* again with Léon Espinosa as her partner.

Hippolyte Monplaisir enjoyed an extensive and fruitful career as a choreographer. After further engagements in America and in Portugal, he returned to Milan and staged a long series of ballets at La Scala. *Benvenuto Cellini* was the first work he created for the great Italian opera house, in 1861. Others included *Nostradamus, Tersicore sulla Terra, La Devadacy,* and *Brahma.* The fabulous technician Amalia Ferraris danced the title role in his *La Camargo,* based on the life of the great French ballerina. Hippolyte Monplaisir had choreographed more than a dozen ballets for La Scala before his final production, *Loreley,* in 1877.

Julia Turnbull was still playing the dramatic version of *Esmeralda* in America in 1857. The ballet was danced in New York as late as 1869, when lovely young Giuseppina Morlacchi, a recent graduate of the ballet school at La Scala (where she must have known Monplaisir) produced it with her own company at Wood's Museum. These were minor efforts, in comparison with the lavish scale of the Monplaisir production.

—*Dance Magazine,* October 1954.

Léon Espinosa from the lithograph by F. D'Avignon in 1857.
(Harvard Theatre Collection)

XIV: Léon Espinosa in America

T HE POSITION of importance occupied by the Espinosa family, for so many years, in the English dance world, lends particular interest to the adventures of the founder of the dynasty, Léon Espinosa, who was perhaps the greatest dancer of them all. In the fascinating account of his career, written by his son, space permitted the inclusion of only one paragraph concerning his extensive appearances in America.

It was exactly a century ago, on September 23, 1850, that Léon Espinosa made his New York debut, at The Astor Place Opera House, in the ballet *Ondine.* The occasion was the first American appearance of a French ballet company which had been imported by Max Maretzek, the leading operatic impresario of New York at that time. In addition to Espinosa, it was headed by Mlle. Célestine Franck, who had appeared at the Paris Opéra, her sister Victorine, a Miss Emily Waldegrave, who had danced with the Monplaisir Ballet, M. Emile Gredelue, who had worked under Jean Petipa's direction in Bordeaux, and Mlle. Espinosa, advertised as from the Porte St. Martin, Paris, who must have been Léon's sister.

The debut of this company was an event of some importance, and in the review it was Espinosa who got the lion's share of the attention. The anonymous critic of the *Spirit of the Times,* a popular theatrical journal, wrote: "M. Léon Espinosa is a man of small stature, well formed, and remarkably nimble. He reminds us of the great Gabriel Ravel by his drolleries, his activity, and the seeming flexibility of his limbs. He performs some very extraordinary feats 'on the light fantastic toe,' and with such ease and agility that he preserves his character as a dancer . . ."

Figaro, another theatrical journal, gave an even more vivid description of the new dancer, but disapproved of his appearance in a classic rôle:

. . . The curtain rises on the ballet, and forth from the door of a cottage darts the most unique and singular figure ever seen on any stage except that of "Punch," of whom M. Léon Espinosa is a wonderful miniature likeness. Nose, eyes, and legs! Such a nose—ye gods! It is a nose and a half. The Duke of Wellington's grafted on the outer edge of Seguin's; then his eyes—black glass eyes! And his legs—the legs of a marionette! We began to believe Punch had arrived in propria persona . . .

With such an apparition before us , it was hard to bring our judgment to bear upon the talent of the artist, but soon that expressive action of M. Espinosa satisfied us that as a comic pantomimist he has few equals. When the ballet ended we ranked him second only to M. Gabriel Ravel, and regretted exceedingly that his peculiar talent should have been so injudiciously misplaced as it was in making him as the lover of Ondine, dance with Mlle. Célestine Franck in the grand pas de deux, instead of remaining throughout, the buffo of the piece. It was as absurd as 'twould be to see Romeo dance a clog hornpipe with Juliet, or to hear Norma sing "Jenny Get Your Hoe Cake Done."

Mlle. Célestine Franck is, without doubt, the most fascinating danseuse we have had in this country; she has not the talent as a dancer of Fanny Elssler, nor as a pantomimist, of Blangy, but she is young, fresh, fair and beautifully formed . . . and she has evidently been educated in the most modern French school. Her poses were beautiful, and the firmness of her step, the rapidity and aplomb of her pirouettes remarkable . . . Figaro believes that Mlle. Célestine Franck will provide the most popular and attractive dancer in the United States until Cerito (sic) arrives;[1] but he protests against M. Léon Espinosa as her partner in a grand pas de deux—he destroys all she does even when he achieves wonders—in character dances they are alike excellent, but as well might Jenny Lind and W. Chapman sing duets, one serious and the other comic, and expect to harmonise, as Mlle. Franck and M. Espinosa do justice to a grand pas de deux . . .

Evidently Espinosa, or the management, took *Figaro's* criticism to heart, for we have found no other review which mentions his appearance in a classical rôle, although he progressed from one triumph to another in comedy and character parts. In a ballet called *Les Meuniers,* which had been given in the United States, some years earlier, by the Ravel family, he won further praise:

The part originally sustained by M. Gabriel Ravel was on this occasion most ably sustained by M. Léon Espinosa, whose flexibility of limb, wonderful activity and peculiarly graceful and unique style of acting elicited very hearty and well deserved applause, intermingled with peals of laughter. We always considered Gabriel Ravel one of the most perfect comedians we ever saw; his acting was as great in its way as that of Edmund Kean, and his power over the muscles of his face enabled him to portray by a look every sensation and passion, from simple wonder to despair. In this respect only is M. Espinosa his inferior, but as a pantomimist, vaulter, and gymnast, he is, we believe, the equal, and as a dancer, the superior of the great Gabriel himself. Need we say more to express our belief that M. Espinosa is a very clever fellow?

Other ballets in the repertoire of the Franck Ballet Company, as it was later known, included *La Déesse de la Danse, Un Mariage Chinois, La Sicilienne*, and *Le Diable à Quâtre.* Of the last ballet, *Figaro* wrote: ". . . M. Espinosa acquitted himself very well in his representation of the drunken basket maker, and also as the *Maître de Danse*, where Célestine was most successful in her transition from awkwardness to the very poetry of motion . . ."

After successful appearances in Boston and Philadelphia, and a return engagement in New York, the Franck Ballet, with Espinosa still prominently featured, departed on a long tour which took them as far south as New Orleans, and west to St. Louis, on the Mississippi River, then a real frontier town.

According to Ann Barzel, writing in *Dance Index*,[2] Espinosa "was captured by Indians in the Rocky Mountains and was to be executed, but he conveyed to his captors through mime that he could show them that he danced better than they did. They allowed him to demonstrate, and he escaped during the dance." It is a picturesque story, and although we have found no mention of his appearances west of the Rockies, source materials for the early west are almost impossible to find; Espinosa was an audacious traveller, and may well have carried his art even as far as the Pacific coast.

Back in New York in the summer of 1851, Espinosa volunteered to dance at the benefit performance of the American dancer, George W. Smith. A ballet called *The Jolly Millers* (probably the same as *Les Meuniers* mentioned above) was produced for the occasion, with the French ballerina, Mlle. Albertine as Colette, Smith as Colin, and Espinosa as Nicais. Smith had a profound admiration for the extraordinary Espinosa, and many years later, in an interview, spoke of this brief association with him as one of the highlights of his career.

Mlle. Franck and most of her associates had apparently returned to Europe, for Espinosa now joined a company headed by Mlle. Hilariot and M. Vegas, who specialised in Spanish character dances, and had appeared in Paris and New Orleans. Espinosa seems to have brought with him part of the repertoire of his former group, for the new ballet company also presented *The Jolly Millers, La Déesse de la Danse,* and *Le Diable à Quâtre.* "Our small but largely funny friend Espinosa is the *droll*," commented the *Spirit of the Times*, "and there is no one like him on this continent for genuine humour." Before they disbanded in the spring of 1852, this company travelled through the south, visiting Charleston, Nashville, Mobile, and other cities.

In May, 1852, the enterprising manager of the St. Louis Theatre, Joseph M. Field, gathered together a ballet *ensemble* which was for nearly a year an integral part of his stock company. It is amazing to realise that nearly a century ago a tiny frontier town like St. Louis, on the very borders of the Indian territory, had a permanent ballet headed by Espinosa, who had been a pupil of Coulon, Coralli, Filippo Taglioni, and Lucien Petipa, with Giovanna Ciocca, a former pupil of Carlo Blasis, as prima ballerina, Giuseppe Carese, who had partnered Nathalie Fitzjames, as *premier danseur*, and, as soloists, several European dancers from the French theatre in New Orleans; Mlle. Winther, Mlles. E. and C. Baron, Charles Winther, and Leon Rabelli. Some day the story of this pioneer ballet company in the remote interior of America should be written in full. When their season finally closed, after about eight months of continuous performances, Léon Espinosa apparently returned to Europe.

He next danced in New York in 1856, when he appeared at the Broadway Theatre as co-star, with Mme. Adèle Monplaisir, of the Ravel family's production of the ballet *Esmeralda*. A crowded and brilliant house welcomed him back to America. Both featured artists were highly praised, a few days later, in *Frank Leslie's Illustrated Newspaper:*

. . . Mme. Monplaisir, as Esmeralda, displayed all that graceful and elegant agility for which she is so famed. The finished beauty of her poses, and the dashing vigour of her *tours de force*, were the themes of general comment and admiration. M. Léon Espinosa is the most admirable buffo dancer we ever saw. He seems double jointed all over, and his features seem capable of every possible humorous distortion. In his way, he is a superb artist, and his performances were received with shouts of laughter and applause . . .

This time Espinosa's stay in the United States was a brief one. He was soon called back to Paris, where for many years he was the brightest star at the Théâtre de la Porte St. Martin. He visited America again in 1890, when he staged the dances for the opening of Madison Square Garden, but that was long after the close of his own career as a dancer.

—Dancing Times, March 1951.

[1]Fanny Cerrito never arrived to dance in America—I.G.

[2]"European Dance Teachers in the United States," by Ann Barzell, in Dance Index, Vol. III, Nos. 4-5-6, April-June, 1944, p. 66.

Giuseppina Morlacchi. (Dance Collection, The New York Public Library)

XV: Ballerina and Plainsman: Giuseppina Morlacchi and Texas Jack

WHEN Buffalo Bill and Texas Jack arrived in Chicago in the autumn of 1872, to begin their first venture in the theatre, they were perhaps the two most flagrantly incompetent gentlemen ever to be engaged as "stars" because of the box-office value of their names. Fresh from the Western plains, where they had won considerable fame because of their prowess in capturing buffalo, wild horses, bandits, and Injuns, they had scarcely seen a play, and had certainly never appeared in one. It was Ned Buntline who had enticed them out of the comparative peace of the Wild West and into the glare of the limelight. Buntline had already won considerable success in New York with the stories and plays he had built around the character of Buffalo Bill. He was convinced that a small fortune could be gathered by presenting Bill Cody on the stage.

Hitherto the Indian fighter had simply laughed at the idea. His best friend, Texas Jack, was easier to convince. He even showed signs of stage fever. It was he who finally persuaded Cody to accept Buntline's strange proposal. Fate must have been prompting Jack, for in the world of the threatre he was to find a wife as well as a career.

The would-be matinée idols arrived in Chicago somewhat unexpectedly. Buntline had not actually believed that they would come. As a matter of fact, he had made not the slightest preparation for their debut. That insignificant circumstance, however, did not worry him in the least.

His first move was the engagement of a press agent, one Major John M. Burke, an old admirer of Bill Cody who later became his manager and life-long friend. Next he rented a theatre, stipulating the following Monday as opening night. When Bill and Jack learned that they were to appear in less than a week, they became somewhat panicky.

"What will we have to do?" they asked anxiously. "Will we have to make long speeches?"

Buntline scratched his head reflectively. "Well, as a matter of fact," he admitted, "I don't know. The play isn't written yet. But don't worry, I can write it tomorrow morning. In the afternoon I'll hire the company."

He dashed off *The Scouts of the Prairie* in four hours. A cynical critic remarked that, considering the literary merit of the piece, he didn't see why it had taken so long. This little quip failed to prevent the triumphant success of the play.

That afternoon Buntline gave Bill and Jack their respective parts, and locked them in their suite at the hotel with instructions to learn their roles before he returned. Then he went out to engage a supporting cast. The two cowboys, left alone with a formidable pile of manuscript, tackled their task with grim determination.

Buntline returned a few hours later, elated at the unexpected success of his search. He had just engaged as featured artist the celebrated ballerina Giuseppina Morlacchi, whose twinkling toes were the toast of New York. What is more, she had agreed not only to dance, but to undertake her first speaking part, that of the Indian maiden Dove Eye.

"And now that that's settled, boys," Buntline concluded, "let's hear how you are getting along with your parts."

Texas Jack volunteered to try first. Rising and assuming a properly impressive attitude, he proceeded to declaim his role in stentorian tones. He began at the beginning and plowed on without pause. Cues, entrances and exits, and stage business just didn't exist. Since he showed every indication of proceeding in this original manner to the end of the drama, Buntline was obliged to interrupt him.

"Wait a minute," he protested. "Don't you know that this is *dialogue*? You say a line and Bill answers you. Dove Eye comes in, and so on—"

Puzzled and hurt, Bill and Jack ruefully admitted that they had not understood these delicate refinements of the dramatic art.

"Gosh, we never talked like this anyway," muttered Bill protestingly. "It would take me six months to learn all this stuff. Come on, let's go back and fight Injuns."

But Texas Jack was still stage-struck. Once more he and Buntline explained the desirability of becoming an actor. Bill stayed.

Buntline saw that it would take some stiff coaching to whip the two plainsmen into presentable dramatic material by Monday. He decided to take Bill in hand himself. Seeking for a similar coach for Texas Jack, he hit upon the dancer Morlacchi. It was true that she didn't know much about diction and delivery, and her English had more than a hint of an Italian accent, but her experience on the stage was long and varied, and the exigencies of the situation made it necessary to seize on any straw.

Next day, at the theatre, Buntline introduced Bill, Jack, and press-agent Burke to Mlle. Morlacchi. She was a small and dainty creature, with expressive dark eyes and delicate, refined features which left one completely unprepared for the Latin fire of her temperamental dancing. Not without reason had she been selected, four years earlier, to introduce the exicting *Can-Can* to conservative Boston.

Buffalo Bill was married, and loyally devoted to his wife. Both Burke and Texas Jack, however, fell promptly and completely under the spell of the adorable little dancer. It was Jack, handsome, hot-headed, and youthful—he was just about Morlacchi's own age—who appealed to the ballerina. Some time later the broken-hearted Burke poured out his sorrows to Mrs. Cody. She has described the scene in her book on the life of Buffalo Bill:

" 'Mrs. Cody,' he had said one night as we sat backstage watching a performance, 'I have met a god and a goddess in my life. The god was Buffalo Bill. . . . The goddess was Mlle. Morlacchi. But I can't have her, Mrs. Cody. I wouldn't be the man I want to be if I tried. Jack's a better man—he's fought the West, and he's had far more hardships than I've ever seen and—and—he deserves his reward. I'll never love any other woman, but there's one thing I can do, I can turn all my affection from the goddess to the god, and so help me, I'll never fail from worshipping him!' "

Major Burke was as good as his word. For the rest of his life he served Buffalo Bill as agent, general factotum, and eulogistic biographer. He acted also as the theatrical representative of Mlle. Morlacchi, whom he continued to adore—from a respectful distance.

The Scouts of the Prairie opened in Chicago, as scheduled, after only four days of rehearsals. In the middle of the first act Buffalo Bill went completely haywire. The fearless Indian fighter forgot his lines entirely, and stood trembling in the middle of the stage.

"Where you have been all this time, Bill?" ad-libbed Buntline, in desperation.

"I've been out on a hunt with Milligan!" Cody burst out impetuously, naming a popular Chicago sportsman. This happy inspiration saved the day. For the rest of the act Buffalo Bill improvised with a spontaneity and wit that would have done credit to a Will Rogers. This was so effective that he continued to do it through the long and successful run of the play.

Debonair Texas Jack came through his ordeal with less agony— possibly because his role called for the pleasurable stage business of making love to Dove Eye. It was becoming increasingly evident that his intentions towards the charming young lady were decidedly serious.

It would be difficult to imagine two lovers with more widely differing backgrounds. Morlacchi—"peerless Morlacchi," the late Philip Hale, who saw her in his salad days, called her—was born in Milan in October, 1843. When she was six years old she was entered as a pupil in the famous ballet school of the La Scala Opera. At that time the prima ballerina was, incredibly enough, a girl from Philadelphia, Augusta Maywood, who had made a successful debut at the Paris Opéra and later gone to Milan. Perhaps it was her presence in the company which first inspired the little Italian dancer with the desire to visit America.

Morlacchi made her New York debut on October, 23, 1867, in *The Devil's Auction*, a ballet spectacle which had been produced as a rival attraction to the famous *Black Crook*. On the night of Morlacchi's arrival in New York the orchestra of the theatre serenaded her with Strauss waltzes and operatic airs, beneath the windows of her suite in the Fifth Avenue Hotel. The manager, with a keen perception of the publicity value of his move, insured her legs for $100,000, so "la Morlacchi is more valuable than *Kentucky!*" (finest race-horse of the day) as a sporting paper commented.

Her debut was a triumph. "Mlle. Morlacchi is a beautiful creature, and she came upon the stage like a sudden ray of light," wrote an anonymous critic in the *New York Tribune*. "She is of the spiritual order of woman, small, delicate, fiery, with a fine little head and a luminous face, and she dances with all her soul as well as with all her body. . . ."

Before her appearance in *The Scouts of the Prairie* Morlacchi had danced all over the eastern United States. She was particularly popular in Boston, where she introduced the French *Can-Can* early in 1868. An eye-witness of her performances there, writing to the Boston *Herald* some forty years after the event, described her performance as a sort of glorified strip-tease, in which five brunettes, headed by Mlle. Morlacchi, and five blondes, captained by Mlle. Diani, unwound and discarded their frilled muslin skirts until they stood only in tights and military headdresses. A contemporary print of Morlacchi in the *Can-Can*, however, shows her in conventional ballet costume and a classic pose. Whatever sort of dance it may have been, the "original Morlacchi *Can-Can*" certainly brought fame and fortune to its creator. It seems that Walt Disney did not invent *The Seven Dwarfs*, either, for in 1869 Morlacchi danced in a ballet of that name, achieving a run of five weeks (as good as the Music Hall's record for the movie!).

The little ballerina had plenty of faith in her ability to earn her own living. When she was at the height of her popularity in Chicago, a spendthrift dandy named Jim Fisk took to following her about. Backstage one evening, just before her entrance, he slipped an enormous diamond ring on her finger. Her music was just beginning, and Morlacchi had no chance to refuse it at the moment. Later she sent for Fisk, and coldly returned his gift. Fisk, a little startled by such a show of virtue in a ballerina, thought that she had misjudged the value of his offering.

"My dear young lady," he explained, "I don't think you quite realize the value of that little stone. It's of the first water, and worth at least $5,000."

Giuseppina shrugged her pretty shoulders. "Bah!" she said carelessly, "I can earn that with one of my toes."

Fisk retired baffled. Later he was overheard to remark, "Now there's a good woman that a bad man can fight for!"

Texas Jack evidently thought so too. Handsome, eccentric, reckless, and a bit wild, he held an irresistible fascination for the little dancer. His life had been the exact antithesis of hers, for it had been spent in the rough, free life of the plains, instead of in the confining, hothouse atmosphere of ballet school and theatre. Born in Virginia, he had gone West alone, when he was just a boy. During the four years of the Civil War he had served as a Scout under a Texas general of the Confederate army. He had been a cowboy, a trapper, a hunter, a rancher, and a government scout.

He had once brought about the capture of a whole gang of border bandits who called themselves "The Lone Star Knights." By winning their confidence and actually living in their camp, he was able to learn their plans and to save a whole pack train of government supplies which they had plotted to capture. On another occasion, when he was out on a solitary hunting expedition, Jack was attacked by hostile Indians. He scalped four of them and acquired several arrow wounds before he decided that discretion was the better part of valor, and beat a hasty retreat. It was a miracle that he escaped with his life.

Even his name, "Texas Jack," had been acquired in romantic fashion. He had been christened John B. Omahundro. One night in Santa Fe he was obliged to beat up Kansas Kit in order to enjoy the privilege of dancing with his girl. After the brawl was over it was suggested that a tongue-twister like Omahundro was scarcely a fitting name for such a hard-fighting son of the prairies. A bottle of whiskey was cracked over his skull, and he was rechristened "Texas Jack."

One can easily imagine the fascination which such tales must have held for a ballerina whose sheltered life had been passed in tedious exercises and endless rehearsals. At any rate, Morlacchi was quick to return the passion of the handsome plainsman. They were married in Boston, where The Scouts of the Prairie had paused during its long road tour, just a few months after their meeting.

So long as the two were appearing together in the play, all went well with this strange alliance. But no sooner was the theatrical season over than Texas Jack felt the call of the wild again. In a few days he was off for the plains of western Nebraska with Buffalo Bill. Morlacchi's life henceforth must have been one of considerable uncertainty. Her husband seems to have been constitutionally allergic to discipline, matrimonial or otherwise. He returned in the autumn, to be sure, and helped to organize the theatrical enterprise of Cody & Omahundro. But a little later he was off again, this time to hunt in the Yellowstone country as guide to the Earl of Dunraven. Next he decided to act as his wife's manager, and presented her in the old classic opera-ballet *La Bayadère* in Boston, in the spring of 1875. When Buffalo Bill organized his famous "Wild West" show, Texas Jack followed suit with one of his own, which he took on tour to South Africa. One of the members of that company was the "Cherokee Kid"—Will Rogers.

Later, when gold was discovered in Colorado, Texas Jack caught the mining fever. It was in Leadville that he died, of pneumonia on June 28, 1880. Giuseppina, who adored him in spite of his erratic wanderings and his frequent inconstancies, had followed him to Colorado and was with him when he died.

Later Morlacchi returned to the east and retired with her sister to a modest home in East Billerica, Massachusetts. When she died in 1886, at the early age of forty-three, the whole town went into mourning, the principal stores were closed, and the dancer of the *Can-Can* was attended to her grave by the clergymen of the Methodist, Baptist, and Roman Catholic churches.

—Dance, September 1942.

Enrico Cecchetti in *Scheherazade*. (Dance Collection, The New York
Public Library)

XVI: Enrico Cecchetti: 1850-1928 — Dancer and Teacher

PART I: THE DANCER

IN ST. PETERSBURG, towards the close of the last century, there was a pleasure garden called the Arcadia, whose outdoor theatre often featured Italian dancers. It was there that the artists of the Russian Imperial Ballet were first dazzled by the technique of a handsome young Italian named Enrico Cecchetti.

A pupil of Lepri, who in turn had inherited the mantle of the great teacher Carlo Blasis, Cecchetti was past master of all the spectacular tricks of his trade. Eight pirouettes were easy for him, in a day when the Russian dancers were quite satisfied with three or four. A Russian critic called him a "bone-splitting specialist of vertiginous dexterity."

Remembered today primarily as the teacher of such renowned artists as Anna Pavlova and Vaslav Nijinsky, Cecchetti was originally noted as a dancer, and a virtuoso of extraordinary skill. At a time when the male dancer was universally neglected, his presence tolerated only when he was absolutely necessary as a prop for the prima ballerina, Cecchetti managed to establish himself as a star dancer in his own right, and even—to judge by London advertisements which featured his name prominently—a definite box-office attraction.

Those who think of Cecchetti solely as a pedagogue, and a strict one, are inclined to forget that Cecchetti was completely a man of the theatre. The son of two dancers, he was, quite literally, born in one—the Tordinona, in Rome, in 1850—and even in his old age he created important mimed roles with the Diaghilev Ballet. The drudgery of the classroom was always, with Cecchetti, a means to an end: he was interested in performance, in the richest sense of the word.

Enrico Cecchetti began performing at the age of five, making his debut in Rota's ballet *Il Giocatore*. Since his parents, Cesare and Serafina

Cecchetti, were dancers, it was natural that they should think of little Enrico whenever children were needed, as frequently happened, in the long, complicated, pantomimic Italian ballets in which they danced.

Enrico was seven years old when, in 1857, his parents came to America as featured members of the Ronzani Ballet, one of the first large-scale ballet companies to appear in the United States. The company had been specially formed, in Italy, to appear as the opening attraction for a brand-new opera house, the Philadelphia Academy of Music. This same theatre, with its oldfashioned "rake"—a sloping stage built in the manner of European theatres of the nineteenth century—is still familiar to the dancers of today's ballet companies.

In 1857, the Academy of Music was the last word in theatrical splendour, and for its first season Ronzani had prepared a number of elaborate, full-length ballets. In one of these, *Il Biricchino di Parigi* (The Gamin of Paris), Enrico Cecchetti made his American debut. He played Ottavio, a youngster who, escaping the surveillance of his nursemaid, leaps upon a parapet overlooking the Seine, and promptly falls into the river, to be rescued by the "hero," the orphan boy Giuseppe (played by Teresina Pratesi, in *travesti*). One of little Enrico's duties, in the third act, was to spring into the arms of the lovely Teresina and smother "him" with kisses and caresses.

The Cecchettis toured the United States for almost a year, and before it was over Enrico was appearing with his older sister, Pia, in a pas de deux, the *Styrien,* interpolated in the ballet *Theresa, the Orphan of Geneva.* In his old age Enrico often used to recall with amusement the primitive theatres and difficult conditions under which they sometimes appeared while pioneering in America.

When the family returned to Italy, Enrico had already made up his mind to become a dancer. His parents did not approve of the youngster's decision, and placed him in a private school to obtain a formal education. But Enrico sabotaged their plans by spending all his spare time practicing pirouettes instead of studying history or mathematics. Finally, when he was thirteen, he persuaded his father to let him enter the ballet academy of Giovanni Lepri, in Florence. His progress there was so rapid that only three years later he made his formal debut, in his father's ballet *Nicolo di Lapi.*

At twenty, with four years of professional experience already behind him, he made his debut as first dancer at La Scala, Milan, in *La Dea del Walhalla*, a ballet by Pasquale Borri, the favorite pupil of Carlo Blasis. Young Cecchetti's initial performance was marked by two memorable incidents. At his entrance, he shocked the audience by falling flat on his back. A little later, he astounded them by executing a flawless series of thirty-two *pirouettes à la seconde,* a feat which no dancer had previously attempted. It was a sensation.

News of his amazing virtuosity spread fast. Whenever a manager wished to engage him, he would also try to obtain a contract for his favorite partner, his sister Pia. He was not always successful, in her behalf, and she soon gave up dancing for marriage. After her retirement Enrico danced with the greatest ballerinas of Italy, including Virginia Zucchi (so vividly described in Alexandre Benois' *Reminiscences of the Russian Ballet*), Giovannina Limido, Malvina Cavallazzi, Adelina Rossi, Pierina Legnani and Carlotta Brianza. Among those of his letters now preserved at the Harvard Theatre Collection there is one in which he speaks of Rosita Mauri, who later became étoile of the Paris Opéra: "... I know Mauri, she is a fine artist (*una artista bravissima*) and I would be proud to be her partner . . ." A little later, he reveals the quite human desire for a good salary to supplement the artistic satisfaction of an engagement: "... Certainly I will never be the dancer to accept the salary of a Grassi, but since I am anxious to return to Milan my demands will have to be limited . . ." (Grassi was a mediocre dancer who had appeared for one season as Zucchi's partner at La Scala.)

Cecchetti made his first appearance in St. Petersburg in 1874, and returned there every season for seven years, dancing in summer theatres. In the winter he toured the length and breadth of Italy. A handsome young fellow with dashing moustachios, he was a special favorite at the Teatro San Carlo in Naples.

In 1885 Cecchetti first danced in London, in the spectacular ballet *Excelsior,* a gigantic production which depicted the scientific progress of the age. Its various scenes showed the discovery of electricity and its application as power (here there was an ensemble of telegraph messengers!), the opening of the Suez Canal, and the emancipation of slaves. The critic of the London *Times* declared "... the dancing left nothing to be desired . . . and Signor Cecchetti expresses the feelings of a newly-liberated slave with remarkable agility . . ." Another observer wrote in the *Illustrated Sporting and Dramatic News*: "... The lean and lissom *primo ballerino* Enrico Cecchetti not only fairly astounds by his wondrous pirouetting, but dances throughout in such finished and graceful styles as fairly to conquer the prejudices I have generally entertained against the masculine ballet dancer. . ."

In the same year Cecchetti, whose negotiations for a return to La Scala had always broken down over the question of salary (he was able to earn much more money in Russia, England and Austria) finally returned to the famous Milan opera house, where he danced for three successive seasons, creating leading roles in such ballets as *Messalina, Gretchen,*

Rolla, and the famous *Amor*, which like *Excelsior*, was choreographed by Luigi Manzotti. In this ballet Cecchetti danced the double role of "a Satyr" and "the Spirit of Glory." *Amor*, like *Excelsior*, *Rolla*, and Manzotti's other ballets, was conceived on the scale of a Hollywood production. It had enormous ensemble dances, ceremonial marches, and magnificent processions; even elephants and camels paraded across the vast stage of La Scala. Occasionally these displays would be briefly interrupted while Cecchetti dazzled the audience with a display of technical fireworks.

Cecchetti was back in Russia in the summer of 1887, dancing at the Arcadia Theatre. This time Marius Petipa took Vsevolojsky, director of the Maryinsky Theatre, to see the brilliant Italian. Considerably impressed, Vsevolojsky offered him a contract with the Russian Imperial Ballet. He made his debut that same season, dancing with Varvara Nikitina in *The Tulip of Haarlem*. Later he partnered Zucchi in *L'Ordre du Roi*, and in the following year, he was appointed second *maître de ballet*.

The climax of Cecchetti's career as a dancer came with the first production of Tchaikowsky's ballet *The Sleeping Beauty*, in 1890, when Cecchetti, at the age of forty, created both the mime role of the Fairy Carabosse and the classical role of the Bluebird. Rumor has it that Petipa allowed him to arrange his own variation in the famous pas de deux. If this is true, he certainly did not spare himself; it bristles with technical hazards, in its double *cabrioles, entrechats-six* and double *tours*. When he again appeared in London, a few years later, he was billed as "the first dancer of the world."

Cecchetti's career as a teacher is another story, but after his first retirement from the stage the great dancer was to return to create a number of memorable roles for Diaghilev. He was the first to play the Old Showman in *Petrouchka*, the Astrologer in *Le Coq d'Or*, Kostchei in *Firebird*, the Chief Eunuch in *Scheherazade*, Lammon in *Daphnis and Chloe*, and the Marquis di Lucca in *The Good-Humored Ladies*. Arnold Haskell has declared Cecchetti's miming as the Shopkeeper in *La Boutique Fantasque* to be the finest he has ever seen.

In 1913 Cecchetti left the Diaghilev company to tour with his favorite pupil, Anna Pavlova, With her he returned to America for the first time since his childhood visit nearly sixty years earlier. After a season however, he went back to the Diaghilev company at the urgent insistence of Vaslav Nijinsky, who preferred his lessons to those of any other teacher.

Cecchetti's favorite role at this period was Pantalon in Fokine's *Carnaval*, a "brisk, lovable little lady-killer of uncertain age," as Cyril Beaumont has described him. If Cecchetti ever complained of overwork, Diaghilev, knowing his weakness for Pantalon, would offer to relieve him of this role. Cecchetti would instantly forget his fatigue and his grievances;

he refused to be deprived of Pantalon, although he was close to seventy.

Even in his last post, as director of the ballet school at La Scala, Cecchetti was close to the stage. He never actually retired; his last appearance, as the Old Showman in *Petrouchka*, took place in 1926, just two years before his death. His dance career was probably one of the longest and most brilliant in theatre history: debut at five, climax at forty, final performance at seventy-six!

PART II: THE TEACHER

A SMALL, MIDDLE-AGED ITALIAN sat in a darkened Moscow theatre and watched a young guest dancer whom a mutual friend had brought him to see.

"What do you think of her?" asked the friend, at the end of the performance.

"Tremendously gifted, but her back is weak, and she has several bad technical faults," replied the Italian.

"How long will it take her to correct them?"

"Two or three years."

"Will you teach her?"

So Enrico Cecchetti became the teacher of Anna Pavlova, the young ballerina. She worked with him exclusively for several years; her back grew stronger, and she gradually mastered technical feats which formerly had seemed impossible for one of her delicate physique. Cecchetti has told the story of those days:

"Those lessons were some of the most remarkable that I have given. I could not give her her soul, or her inspiration, but I could give her the benefit of a technique which was strengthening, and which assisted her in expressing herself more freely. She had acquired a trick of pressing her hands on the hips of her ballet skirts, and to correct this, I made her dance in short knickers and a little coat for a whole year. What a marvellous worker she was, how hard she fought to conquer certain defects in her technique! Though, as I have said before, her art is prompted by genius, and mechanical defects could easily be forgiven her, still, she herself had a passion for perfection which stopped at nothing!"[1]

Through the dancing of Anna Pavlova, Cecchetti, who himself had been a great dancer, influenced a whole generation of young artists. Pavlova, however, was only one of his famous pupils. There is hardly a well-known dancer today [*these words were written in 1953—I.G.*] who has not been touched in some way by his magic: those who are too young to have studied with him have worked with his pupils. Even those who are primarily products of the Russian school have been profoundly influenced by Cecchetti's teaching, for he spent a dozen years in Russia and many of his theories and practical ideas about the teaching of classical ballet have been absorbed into the Russian system.

Cecchetti was a fanatic, a man completely and utterly devoted to the art of dancing. He was that rare phenomenon, a superb technician and an artist of genius who was also analytical enough to be a magnificent teacher. World-famous as a performer, Cecchetti was never self-centered enough to concentrate all of his interest and ability in his own dancing. Even as a young man he was generous in sharing his knowledge, and his first pupils were scarcely younger than himself.

Cecchetti was the pupil of Giovanni Lepri, who in turn was the favorite pupil of Carlo Blasis, the great teacher and theoretician who virtually founded the Italian school. Blasis published his first text-book in 1820, before he was twenty-five, and its principles are still applicable today.

Cecchetti's first important pupil was Luigi Albertieri, who by merely watching other dancers had managed to become proficient enough to obtain a professional engagement. Cecchetti saw him dance, one night, and realized that while he had extraordinary natural gifts, he was entirely untrained. He offered to teach him. Albertieri accepted with alacrity, but when after several months of daily work Cecchetti still kept him at the barre for the entire lesson, he finally became restless, and complained. Cecchetti relented: he permitted him to do the same exercises in center floor!

In spite of this harsh corrective diet of barre work, Albertieri persevered. Thanks to Cecchetti's generous help, he made his debut at La Scala, Milan, and eventually came to the United States as *premier danseur* and ballet master of the Metropolitan Opera. Later he opened a school in New York, where he numbered Bentley Stone, Arthur Mahoney, and the late Catherine Littlefield among his pupils.

Cecchetti was a strict—even a harsh—disciplinarian, and on occasion his dissatisfaction with a pupil could drive him into a fury. Nicholas Legat, himself a great teacher, has left an amusing description of Cecchetti chasing Albertieri across the studio, brandishing a cane at him. Half an hour later they were reconciled, with many fervent apologies and embraces. Outside of the ballet studio, Cecchetti could be gentleness itself. He adored animals, especially cats. One of his dance combinations was named the Glissade de Mami, after his favorite pet, a graceful and elegant coal-black puss.

It was as the result of his brilliant success as a dancer at the Maryinsky Theatre, in St. Petersburg, that Cecchetti was appointed one of the teachers in the Imperial Russian Ballet School. Marius Petipa, director of the ballet company, realized that the Italian star had much to offer his Russian dancers, who were noted for their purity of style but not for technical virtuosity. It was Cecchetti, who could turn eight or ten pirouettes with ease, who first taught the Russians the trick of snapping the head during turns, enabling them to pirouette with much greater security and precision, without becoming dizzy. Cecchetti held a special class for the soloists of the company, and among its members were Matilda Kchessinskaia, Lubov Egorova, and Olga Preobrajenska, who were already ballerinas. In their Paris studios, in recent years, they have passed on to pupils like Baronova, Toumanova and Riabouchinska an artistic heritage strongly influenced by the teachings of the Italian master. Among the younger pupils of Cecchetti at the Maryinsky were Tamara Karsavina and Vaslav Nijinsky, who became the greatest stars of the Diaghilev Ballet, Lydia Kyasht, who had a long career in England, and Alexandra Fedorova.

Cecchetti was the favorite teacher of both Nijinsky and Karsavina, and at their special request, the *Maestro* was appointed official teacher of the Diaghilev Ballet when it began its resplendent career in Western Europe. In 1913 Pavlova persuaded Cecchetti to accompany her on an American tour. Before they returned to Europe, Cecchetti began to receive frantic telegrams from Diaghilev: "Come immediately, I need you urgently." Cecchetti replied that he was still under contract to Pavlova. "Beseech Madame Pavlova to release you," pleaded the next wire from Diaghilev. Although he had no desire to break his contract, Cecchetti feared that some dire emergency had arisen. Reluctantly he explained the difficulty to Pavlova. She agreed that he should join Diaghilev in Paris.

There the great impressario took him at once to see a performance of the company. As the evening progressed, Diaghilev pointed out a handsome lad who was dancing in the ensemble. "How long will it take before he can replace Nijinsky?" he asked. Cecchetti, who had already noticed the young man's remarkable talent, replied without hesitation: "Two or three years." Actually, the boy was dancing leading roles long before that length of time had elapsed. Placed in Cecchetti's hands, he worked like a slave, practising for hours every day under the strict and relentless direction of the master. His name was Leonide Massine.

As the official teacher of the Diaghilev Ballet, Cecchetti guided a whole generation of distinguished dancers—dancers who today are artistic leaders all over the world: Alexandra Danilova, Leon Woizikowsky, Anton Dolin, Lubov Tchernicheva, even the baby of the company, little Alicia Markova.

When he was nearly seventy, Cecchetti decided he had had enough of constant touring. Much as he loved the stage—and one of the secrets of his greatness as a teacher lay in the fact that he never lost contact with the living theatre—he decided to settle down in London, open a school and confine his own appearances to the annual visit of the Diaghilev Ballet to the British capital. There was no lack of talent among the English dancers. Those whom he taught there included Ninette de Valois, director of the Sadler's Wells Ballet, Marie Rambert, director of the Ballet Rambert, and Margaret Craske, who teaches young American dancers at the Metropolitan Opera, the Juilliard School, and Jacob's Pillow.

It was while he was teaching in London that Cecchetti agreed to let Cyril W. Beaumont, the noted authority on dance history, codify and publish his method of teaching. With the technical assistance of Stanislas Idzikowski, one of Cecchetti's finest pupils in the Diaghilev Ballet, for the first volume (*The Theory and Practice of Classical Theatrical Dancing*) and of Margaret Craske for the second (*The Theory and Practice of Allegro in Classical Ballet*), Beaumont succeeded in translating into clear and practical terms Cecchetti's great legacy to the dance. [2]

The final chapter of Cecchetti's career as a teacher was enacted in his beloved Italy. He had returned there, at the age of seventy-three, intending to retire. Scarcely had he arrived in Turin when Diaghilev sent him young Serge Lifar, his latest protegé, who was to become the last *premier danseur* of the Diaghilev company, and later, for many years the head of the Paris Opéra Ballet. Next, the directors of La Scala, the great Milan opera house where Cecchetti had danced with such distinction fifty years earlier, heard of his presence and asked him to take charge of the ballet school, which in recent years had been badly neglected. He could not resist such an appealing assignment. His stipulations, however, are evidence of his disinterested devotion to the dance: he insisted that pupils be accepted on the basis of talent, without reference to nationality, that all lessons be free, and that his dancers should never be interrupted (for stage rehearsals, for example) during the hours set aside for class. His conditions were accepted, and in 1925 Cecchetti became director of the La Scala Ballet School. There he taught Gisella Caccialanza, who was a soloist in Balanchine's original American Ballet and later prima ballerina of the San Francisco Ballet, Attilia Radice, who for a score of years was Italy's leading dancer, and Cia Fornaroli Toscanini and Vincenzo Celli. The *Maestro*, faithful to his art, literally, until his last breath, was stricken by his fatal illness while teaching a class of La Scala, just twenty-five years ago, in November, 1928.

Through almost every line of current classical ballet teaching, even the most Russian, Cecchetti "blood," however diluted, has been infused into

American Ballet. Even those who disagree most heartily with the rigidity of his method cannot but be thankful for his magnificent—if not unparalleled—contribution to the art and science of dance teaching.

—*Dance,* September/October 1953.

[1]Olga Racster: *The Master of the Russian Ballet,* pp. 212-213.

[2]A third volume, *The Theory and Practice of Advanced Allegro in Classical Ballet,* by Margaret Craske and Derra de Moroda was published in 1956.

A James Montgomery Flagg drawing of the wings of the Metropolitan Opera during the 1915-16 season, with ballet mistress Pauline Verhoeven and premiers Rosina Galli and Giuseppe Bonfiglio.

XVII: The Metropolitan Opera Ballet, 1883-1951

THE METROPOLITAN OPERA BALLET has never been able to build up a consistent, uninterrupted tradition, nor to develop an individual style as, for example, the Paris Opéra Ballet has done. Founded in 1883, when the brilliance of the romantic ballet had faded and the present renaissance of the dance was yet undreamed, the Metropolitan Opera Company had no great incentive for the foundation of a permanent, artistically important ballet group. Established in an age when song was preeminent, the Metropolitan has devoted itself fairly consistently to its glorification, at the expense of its sister art, the dance.

Nevertheless, ever since its opening the Metropolitan has always maintained some sort of dance company of its own (for long periods it was the only permanent dance group in America); and over the years the Metropolitan Opera Ballet has managed, in spite of the innumerable difficulties of functioning in a subordinate position, to chalk up a modest list of achievements and a few legitimate triumphs.

Among the celebrated dancers and choreographers who have worked with (and sometimes battled against!) the Metropolitan, one finds the names of George Balanchine, Anna Pavlova, Adolph Bolm, Rosina Galli, Luigi Albertieri, Ruth Page, Boris Romanoff, Cia Fornaroli Toscanini, Adeline Genée, Malvina Cavallazzi, Bianca Froehlich, Mikhail Mordkin, Rita De Leporte, Felia Doubrovska, Ruthanna Boris, George Chaffee, Maria Gambarelli, Anatole Vilzak, Marina Svetlova, William Dollar, Lew Christensen, and countless others, famous in their day, whose names have faded into the past.

Among the ballets danced by the Metropolitan's own forces during the regular opera seasons (exclusive of the special seasons given at this theatre by various ballet companies) have been *Petrouchka, Le Coq d'Or, Coppélia,* and two American ballets, John Alden Carpenter's *Skyscrapers* and Henry Gilbert's *The Dance in Place Congo.* The Metropolitan Ballet even collaborated, back in the dark days of the 'nineties, on the production of a big historical ballet spectacle, *America*, patterned after the famous old Italian classic, *Excelsior*.

When the brand-new Metropolitan Opera House opened its doors in the autumn of 1883, its ballet was headed by Malvina Cavallazzi, one of the distinguished dancers of her day, and a former prima ballerina of La Scala in Milan. Cavallazzi managed to hold her own against the superb voices of the golden age of opera. Describing her, a contemporary critic lapsed into unaccustomed rhapsodies:

> She is music embodied in visible motion. She flits across the stage like a flower on the wind. Invisible wings seem to bear her hither and thither with swiftness and lightness incredible, and every pose is a sculptor's dream. Our gay grandsires love to talk of Fanny Elssler, of Taglioni, of Cerrito. They are obliged to confess that they find in Madame Cavallazzi the perfect modern representative of the supreme heroines of the Terpsichorean art. She is one of the few exquisite *artistes* who elevated the dance from the somewhat vulgarized ballet to its legitimate place in the realms of poetry. As première danseuse in such operas as *Robert le Diable*, *Favorita*, *Carmen*, *Aida*, *La Traviata*, and *Mefistofele*, she fairly divides the honors with prima donnas and tenors. Indeed, there are occasions when she is the bright particular star of the evening. . .

One such occasion was her appearance in the mimed role of Fenella, the dumb girl, in Auber's opera *Masaniello*. "The most emphatic success of the evening was won by Mme. Cavallazzi, who in the part of Fenella discovered herself as an actress of a great emotional power and deep intelligence," commented the *New York Herald*. "A more picturesque, a more graceful or a more pathetic embodiment of this character, it would be difficult to conceive of . . .," while the *Sun* described her as a "charmingly graceful and touchingly sympathetic Fenella."

Surprisingly enough, none of the papers made note of the fact that, judging by the evidence of a contemporary photograph, Cavallazzi danced the part of the Neapolitan peasant girl in *bare feet*—an appropriate gesture, but certainly an extraordinary one, some twenty years before Isadora Duncan and Ruth St. Denis revolutionized the dance by discarding their ballet slippers!

Unfortunately the reviewers, who had only admiration for the staging and dramatic action of *Masaniello*, found Auber's simple melodies "inane," and it was dropped from the Metropolitan repertoire. Thirty years later Anna Pavlova played Fenella in her only moving picture, *The Dumb Girl of Portici*, based on the same work.

The programs for the Metropolitan's first season make no mention of any choreographer, and it is probable that Cavallazzi arranged her own dances and those of the corps de ballet. A year later a certain M. Baptistin appeared on the scene, as the first Metropolitan ballet master of whom we have record. He brought with him three first dancers, Lucia Cormani, Adele Fallio, and Isolina Torri, who had all been trained at the famous ballet academy of La Scala. The following season found Herr Opfermann "of the Grand Opera House, Frankfort," in charge, while the two ballerinas were Bettina De Sortis, from La Scala, and Maria Bonfanti, a pupil of Carlo Blasis, who had been one of New York's favorite dancers ever since her sensational success in *The Black Crook* some twenty years earlier. With two such accomplished dancers at his disposal, Opfermann undertook the production, early in 1886, of the famed Walpurgis Night Ballet in *Faust*, which Antony Tudor has revived at the Metropolitan this season.

Records of the ballet for these early years are exasperatingly meager, and it has not been possible to discover much about the size or quality of the corps de ballet. In 1885, we learn from the programs, there were at least "16 Ladies of the Corps de Ballet," but critical comment was reserved exclusively for the leading dancers. This was the age when the prima ballerina reigned supreme, and the ensemble was merely an accessory, often composed of dancers who had little or no formal training. The Metropolitan's own ballet school was not inaugurated until 1909, when the company had been in existence for twenty-six years.

In 1886, apparently, an attempt was made to improve the calibre of the corps de ballet, for the prospectus for the season advertised a "Complete Corps de Ballet Selected from London, Berlin, St. Petersburg and New York." (Evidently Russian dancers were not unknown in America even in those days!) That autumn the Metropolitan presented its first independent ballet, *Vienna Waltzes*, described as a "Ballet Divertissement in 3 Tableaux, by Louis Frappart, arranged for the American stage by Signor Ambroggio (who was the Met's choreographer, that season), music arranged by Joseph Bayer." The score consisted of bits and pieces selected from the works of Haydn, Lanner, Johann Strauss, Brahms, and Offenbach. The Viennese adapter, Bayer, is remembered as the composer of *The Fairy Doll*, a ballet popular all over Europe towards the end of the last century, and later given at the Metropolitan. It is still familiar to us as the prototype of *La Boutique Fantasque*, and all the other toy-shop ballets.

Vienna Waltzes seems to have been a rather long-winded affair which included an Austrian village scene, a wedding scene, and a final tableau at the Vienna Exposition of 1873, with world travellers presenting their various national dances: the English, a hornpipe, the Germans, a Ländler, the Hungarians, a Czardas, the French, a Minuet, and the Americans, a Virginia Reel danced to traditional melodies. The featured dancers in this first Metropolitan ballet were Malvina Cavallazzi, a Miss Braithwaite, who was Kathi, the bride, and Fraulein Leonhardt "from the City Theatre, Hamburg," who danced the *travesti* role of Leopold, the bridegroom, and later resumed the garb of her own sex to dance a Spanish Bolero. The choreographer appeared in a mimed role.

Giovanni Ambroggio remained in control of the Metropolitan Ballet until 1890, and although he had the services of several excellent ballerinas, such as the Russian Theodora De Gillert, and Margaretha Urbanska, who had danced in Berlin, he produced no more ballets, while the incidental dances in the operas met with only modest approval, and sometimes not even that. The low estate to which the ballet had fallen is revealed in an article by Gustav Kobbé which appeared in the Metropolitan program itself, in 1888: ". . . The ballet is regarded as having such inherent inconsistency . . . that any effort to make it historically or locally correct is regarded as useless. It is supposed to exist merely for the sake of forming a pretty adjunct to a scene. Therefore the dances and the costumes must be pretty whether they be truthful or not. For instance, when the production of *Ferdinand Cortez* was under discussion, no one for a moment entertained the idea that the faces of the dancers should be stained. Of course some discrimination is had with regard to the colors of the costumes, and there are tambourines for the Spanish dances, palm-leaves for the Orient, and bows and quivers, lances, clubs and tomahawks, for those of savage nations . . ."

Matters improved somewhat upon the engagement of a new choreographer, Augusto Francioli, in the autumn of 1890. The ballet even received some good criticisms. After the première of a new opera, *The Vassal of Szigeth,* the *New York Mail and Express* noted that "The Hungarian ballet is novel and pleasing," while the *Times* conceded that "A word of praise is due to the ballet master for his picturesque arrangement of the dance, which is executed with a precision new to the opera house." Perhaps as the result of this success, Francioli was assigned the staging of an entire ballet, *Dresden China,* which had its first performance on February 4, 1891, and starred a new *première danseuse,* Martha Irmler. The program announced the appearance of Mlles. Leontine, Francioli, Polednik, and Lengyelfy in solo roles, "supported by a complete corps de ballet of 250"!

A notable event of the 'nineties was the presentation at the Metropolitan of the ballet-spectacle *America,* which took an entire evening for its performance, and after its opening on December 5, 1893, was given on alternate nights with the opera, well into the next year. Whether or not *America* may be legitimately called a Metropolitan ballet production is open to question, for Imre Kiralfy, its director, had staged it in the preceding season for the Chicago World's Fair, and brought many of the Chicago performers to New York. However, the Metropolitan corps de ballet certainly participated, while the two prima ballerinas, Edea Santori and Fiordilice Stocchetti (both trained at La Scala) were simultaneously appearing, on the alternate evenings, in *Carmen, Orfeo, Les Huguenots* and other operas of the standard repertoire.

America, a "Grand Historical, Allegorical and Ballet Spectacle," traced the history of the United States from the founding of Plymouth down to the invention of the telephone, telegraph, and electric light. It included a scene in Merrymount, with a Maypole Dance and several variations based on English folk dances, a "Grand Ballet of the Arts and Sciences" and a "grand Ballet of American Inventions." The evening ended with "The Triumph of Columbia" and a "Grand Cortege of the States and Territories of the Union." All of this was obviously suggested by Luigi Manzotti's celebrated spectacle *Excelsior,* first produced at La Scala in 1881, which also glorified the wonders of science and the progress of invention, and concluded with a similar "March of the Nations."

Male dancers had been notoriously absent from the Metropolitan until the debut, on April 17, 1895, of Luigi Albertieri, pupil and protegé of Enrico Cecchetti. He made his first appearance in the skating scene in *Le Prophète* (familiar to us today as Frederick Aston's delightful ballet *Les Patineurs*) and his partner was the fine dancer Maria Giuri, who had danced in Russia and been ballerina at La Scala. A year later Albertieri became ballet master at the Metropolitan, a post which he retained intermittently (Augusto Francioli returned for a couple of seasons) for ten years. Later Albertieri was for a time the choreographer of the Chicago Opera. Upon his retirement from the theatre, in 1915, he opened a studio in New York City, where until his death in 1930 he trained dancers according to the strict methods of his master, Cecchetti.

For one season, 1899-1900, Albertieri had as prima ballerina a Russian dancer, Catherina Bartho, who had studied with Cecchetti in Moscow and then danced her way around the world. When she appeared at the Metropolitan her career had already encompassed a year in Australia, where she was one of the earliest pioneers of classical ballet, and visits to New Zealand, the Samoan Islands, and Hawaii. Bartho loved to dance; she habitually practiced three hours a day in addition to rehearsals and performances, and when an interviewer asked if she actually enjoyed such arduous work, she replied: "It is my only love—my life, my heart. When I am on the stage and the music sounds in my ears I feel as if I was in the clouds . . ." But at the Metropolitan she was given little to do, so she soon continued her eastward journey on to London, where she found greater opportunity.

With the accession of Heinrich Conried as director of the Metropolitan in 1903, the ballet underwent one of its periodic renovations. We have at hand a delightful letter from Mme. Bianca Froehlich, whom he engaged as prima ballerina, describing her five years at the Metropolitan. Viennese by birth, Froehlich had received her training at the State Opera there, and later appeared in Cologne, Germany, where Conried saw her dance. When she signed her contract for New York, Conried authorized her to audition and hire eighteen girls from the Vienna opera, for the Metropolitan ensemble. These were augmented by thirty more, Spanish, Italian, and French, whom he engaged in Europe, and six American girls, retained from the previous season. Choreographers under Conried were Albertieri and Francioli. At that time, good ballet slippers were unobtainable in the United States, and each year a singer in the chorus, who lived in Milan and went home every summer, would take orders from all the dancers and purchase shoes for them wholesale (at less than $1 per pair!) from the famous ballet-slipper maker, Nicolini.

Coppélia was given at the Metroplitan for the first time early in 1904, with Froehlich and another ballerina, Enrica Varasi, alternating as Swanhilda. Frantz was danced in *travesti* by Tekla Braun. A year later this role was taken by Pauline Verhoeven, a Belgian dancer who later returned to the Metropolitan as ballet mistress. On January 28, 1905, Bayer's *The Fairy Doll* was presented, with choreography by Albertieri, and Bianca Froehlich, Enrica Varasi and Vincenzo Romeo in prominent roles.

Froehlich was assigned the thankless task of doubling for the singer Olive Fremstad in the Dance of the Seven Veils for the American première of Richard Strauss' *Salome*. In her own words, "In those early days decorum had to be preserved at all costs, and an Oriental dance that was not permitted one suggestive step, and still had to convey voluptuousness for nearly one half hour, was quite a feat." Even so, the dowagers of the "diamond horseshoe" were so scandalized by *Salome* that it was withdrawn after one performance, and not revived at the Metropolitan until 1934. A happier experience for Froehlich was her appearance in *Die Fledermaus*. Later Bianca Froehlich (using only her first name, Mme. Bianca) taught in Cleveland, Ohio, numbering among her pupils Eleanore Tennis, former partner of Paul Haakon, and Eric Braun of Ballet Theatre.

When Giulio Gatti-Casazza became General Manager of the Metropolitan (a post which he shared with Andreas Dippel for two seasons, before assuming the sole directorship in 1910), he brought with him from Italy a conductor, Arturo Toscanini, a ballerina, Gina Torriani, and a choreographer, Ludovico Saracco. The last-named came from a family long famous in the annals of La Scala, where a relative of his, Giorgio Saracco, had staged Tchaikowsky's *Sleeping Beauty* and Delibes' *Sylvia*. At the same time a Czech dancer, Ottokar Bartik, was engaged to stage and dance in the ballets of Smetana's folk-opera, *The Bartered Bride*. Giuseppe Bonfiglio had joined the company several years earlier; he was to remain its principal male dancer for thirty years, until the retirement of Gatti-Casazza in 1935.

In 1909 an honest effort was made to improve the status of the Metropolitan ballet. Several new soloists were engaged, including Rita Sacchetto, whose pantomimic dances had created something of a sensation in Europe (she later became a star of silent films), Ivy Craske, a young English girl (not related to Margaret Craske, who now heads the opera's ballet school), and Tamara Swirskaia, who later acted with John Barrymore in Tolstoy's *Redemption*. Bayer's old ballet *Vienna Waltzes* was revived, and ballet divertissements were occasionally presented after the opera.

Most important, however, was the establishment that year of the Metropolitan Opera Ballet School. Dancers were still being recruited in Europe, and the management decided that the opening of a school with high professional standards would enable them to engage Americans. For this purpose Malvina Cavallazzi, who since leaving the Metropolitan twenty-two years earlier had danced very successfully at the Empire Theatre, in London, and later had opened a school there, was brought over from England. With her came her secretary and assistant, Kathleen Harding, who was for many years secretary of the Metropolitan Ballet School. In its early years the school offered free training, with the understanding that when they were adequately prepared, the pupils would enter the ballet. Cavallazzi had to work under a great disadvantage, for free students were considered apprentices, and because of child labor laws could not be admitted under the age of sixteen, which is late for the training of a dancer. Even so, each pupil had to have the written permission of his parents or guardians.

The students wore knee-length pink tutus to all classes, and their legs were modestly encased in pink cotton knickers. This enchanting costume was later modified, but until 1935 members of the ballet were required to wear pink silk opera hose and knee-length tunics to all classes and rehearsals. A practise dress which rose even an inch above the knee was cause for a two-dollar fine, deductible from the dancer's salary.

Cavallazzi's work was so successful that after only one year about ten of her pupils were accepted into the ballet. The number was gradually increased until by 1914 it was no longer found necessary to import dancers for the ensemble (which then numbered twenty-four), and a young pupil of Cavallazzi's, Eva Swain, was engaged as the Metropolitan's first American *première danseuse*.

Discussion of the school has led us somewhat ahead of our story. On February 28, 1910, *Coppélia* had been revived for the American debut of no less an artist than Anna Pavlova. Partnered by Mikhail Mordkin, she danced in the Metropolitan's own version of the old classic, staged by the opera's ballet master, Saracco. The overwhelming success of the two magnificent Russian dancers is too well known to require discussion here, but Pavlova and Mordkin appeared with the opera company for two seasons, dancing Mordkin's ballet *Aziade* and a number of divertissements, in addition to *Coppélia*.

Meanwhile a new ballerina, Cia Fornaroli (who, as Mme. Toscanini, taught for many years in New York) had made her debut and, in spite of the severe competition of the Russian stars, earned a marked success which continued in her later career in Italy. In 1912 a new choreographer, Ettore Coppini, came to the Metropolitan, and it was in his version of *Coppélia* that the brilliant Danish dancer Adeline Genée, whose technical precision is said to have been unequalled, made her bow at the opera. She was already very popular in New York, having starred in several operettas here, but this was America's first chance to see her in one of the classics of the ballet, and her success was complete. Unfortunately her stay at the Metropolitan was brief; soon after, she returned to England, where she has been one of the prime forces in the tremendous British renaissance of ballet.

At this period the sixteen-year-old ballerina of the Chicago Opera, Rosina Galli, was causing a furore whenever she appeared. Admirers of the Italian school, as contrasted with the freer Russian style, went so far as to call her the greatest dancer in the world. When she danced in *Carmen*, then sung by Mary Garden, she received more applause than the prima donna—so much more, in fact, that Garden refused to appear again on the same program with her. (Old-timers still rave about the double circle of pirouettes, swift as light, which she executed in the *Carmen* ballet. Perhaps it wasn't authentically Spanish, but it must have been spectacular.)

On the resignation of Eva Swain, the young American girl who had been leading dancer for the season of 1913-14, Galli was engaged for the Metropolitan. Cavallazzi had retired and returned to Italy, and in 1913 Pauline Verhoeven had become both opera choreographer and director of the ballet school.

Conditions in the Metropolitan Ballet under Verhoeven were described by the famous novelist Willa Cather in an article which appeared in *McClure's Magazine* for October, 1913. Mme. Verhoeven, she wrote, found American girls pretty, intelligent, self-confident, and completely unafraid of physical hazard (a quality which has led, more recently, to the development of a number of American dancers distinguished more for athletic prowess than for subtlety of style).

At this time the ensemble dancers received the princely sum of $15 a week during their first year, $18 in the second, and $20 in the third. (As recently as Balanchine's regime, 1935-38, salaries ranged from a minimum of $30 a week for beginners to $50 for soloists, some of them fairly famous ones.)

Mme. Verhoeven's tenure was brief, for she died in 1917. Margaret Curtis, a pupil of Cavallazzi and of Michel Fokine, became the next teacher of the ballet school, remaining in charge until 1950, when it was taken over by Ballet Theatre and its staff, headed by Antony Tudor and Margaret Craske. Among the many successful dancers who had their first ballet lessons with Miss Curtis may be mentioned Nora Kaye and Ruthanna Boris, both of whom made their first stage appearances in the children's ballets of *La Juive* and other operas. After Verhoeven's death Rosina Galli became director of the ballet as well as its prima ballerina. Although she choreographed many of the opera ballets herself, she was assisted at various times by guest choreographers such as Adolph Bolm and Ottokar Bartik, who were called in for specific assignments, as well as August Berger, a veteran Czech ballet master who had worked at La Scala, and Giuseppe Bonfiglio, who relieved her of a great deal of the tedium of rehearsing, although he did no original choreography.

During Galli's first decade at the Metropolitan the ballet basked in the favor of both press and public. It had not enjoyed such enthusiastic approval at any other period, before or since. This extraordinary success was due almost exclusively to the magical artistry of one individual, for there is little reason to believe that the ensemble (although it did have admirable discipline and *esprit de corps*) was anything extraordinary. But for Galli herself there was nothing but the most extravagant praise.

"The sensation of the evening was the brilliant dancing of Rosina Galli, whose performance literally swept the vast audience off its feet," wrote the *N. Y. American* of a performance of *Carmen* in which Geraldine Farrar and Giovanni Martinelli also appeared. "Seldom has a ballerina received such applause." "Of individual performances, that of Rosina Galli surpasses anything done by the singers," said the *N. Y. Mail,* speaking of Granados' opera *Goyescas.* "The prima ballerina is in her element in Spanish dances and interprets the whole spirit of the opera in her few moments on the stage." The *Brooklyn Eagle*, writing of the skating ballet in *Le Prophète*, said: "First and foremost praise must go to little Rosina Galli and her partner Bonfiglio, who in their dancing with the assistance of the entire corps de ballet afforded a riot of color that transcended every one of the singing principals." (These "singing principals," so summarily dismissed, included Matzenauer, Muzio, Didur and one Enrico Caruso.)

So discerning and sensitive a critic as James Huneker wrote of the Italina ballerina: "What of Rosina Galli, whose pedal technique is as perfect as the vocal technique of Miss Hempel, whose mimique is as wonderful in its way as are the hieratic attitudes and patibulary gestures of Mary, the celebrated serpent of Old Nile? Don't we, to a man, adore Rosina? Thunderous affirmations assail the welkin!"

Galli had ample opportunity to shine, for important ballets were given almost every year. The first American production of Borodin's *Prince Igor*, in the season of 1915-16, included the full ballet, choreographed by Ottokar Bartik. (The Diaghilev Ballet, which made its New York appearances under the auspices of the Metropolitan Opera Association as part of its subscription series, presented the Fokine version of *Prince Igor* here in the spring of 1916.) The Walpurgis Night Ballet of *Faust* was revived for Galli in 1917. In the same season Adolph Bolm staged *Le Coq d'Or,* after the original of Michel Fokine, with the singers in the pit, and their roles mimed by dancers on the stage. The cast included Galli, Bolm, Bonfiglio, Bartik, and Queenie Smith, a member of the ballet who later became a musical comedy star on Broadway.

March 23, 1918, saw the première of an American ballet, *The Dance in Place Congo*, which dealt with negro life in New Orleans and had a score by Henry Gilbert. Galli, as Aurore, executed a Voodoo Dance, but Bartik's choreography was critized as being more European than American. The ballet-pantomine *Il Carillon Magico*, composed by Riccardo Pick-Mangiagalli, had choreography by Galli, who was highly praised for the "poetry and pathos" of her interpretation of the role of Pierrot.

At this period almost every opera was given with a complete ballet, most of which were later cut. Verdi's *Don Carlos*, given in 1950 with no dancing at all, then had an elaborate Ballet of the Pearls, and there were big ballets in *Manon, Ernani, Die Loreley* and *Thaïs.*

Stravinsky's *Petrouchka* entered the Metropolitan repertoire in 1919, with choreography by Bolm, after Fokine, and Galli, Bolm, Bonfiglio, Queenie Smith and Florence Rudolph in leading roles.

A severe illness in 1925 caused Galli's temporary retirement. Although she did not dance for nearly two seasons, the ballet continued fairly active. The Broadway dance director Sammy Lee was called in to collaborate on the choreography of a new American ballet, *Skyscrapers*, which had a score by John Alden Carpenter and decor and costumes by Robert Edmond Jones. In *Skyscrapers* the gifted Rita De Leporte, an American dancer who later succeeded Galli as prima ballerina, made her first appearance in a leading role. "White Wings" was danced by Roger Dodge, known for his unique collection of photographs of Vaslav Nijinsky. In the same season Florence Rudolph, a protegé of Galli's who had been called upon to replace her in most of the opera ballets, danced *Petrouchka* with Bolm, Bonfiglio and Bartik, while Armando Agnini, now stage director of the San Francisco Opera Company, mimed the role of the Jolly Merchant.

Galli returned to the stage on March 19, 1927, in the American première of Alfredo Casella's ballet *La Giara,* based on a story by Luigi Pirandello. In addition to dancing the role of Nela, Galli was responsible for the choreography. Meanwhile Ruth Page, later to become ballet mistress of the Chicago Opera, choreographer of *Frankie and Johnny*, and a pioneer force in American ballet, had made her debut as guest soloist in *The Bartered Bride*, later appearing in *Aida, Mignon* and other operas.

After a revival of *Coq d'Or* in 1928, the Metropolitan presented no more independent ballets until Balanchine's regime, which began seven years later. Galli, after her illness, had made no real attempt to regain the spectacular technique which had made her dancing so remarkable, although she continued to dance with superb finesse until her retirement, upon her marriage to Gatti-Casazza, in 1931. Her successor, Rita De Leporte, was a brilliant dancer in quite a different style: light, aerial, mercurial, she would have been splendid in roles like *Firebird* or some of the works of Balanchine. But the Metropolitan, which had suffered a severe blow from the Wall Street crash and the subsequent depression, was barely able to survive the early 'thirties, and its limited budget permitted no expenditures for new ballets. By the time Gatti-Casazza retired and returned to Italy in 1935, taking his wife with him, the opera ballet had become stale and listless from constant repetition of the same "incidental dances," without the incentive of new productions to keep it alive.

Thinking that a new broom would make a clean sweep, Edward Johnson engaged the newly organized American Ballet, directed by George Balanchine, Lincoln Kirstein, and Edward Warburg, to provide the opera ballets. The Metropolitan's own group was disbanded, although a few of its younger members were absorbed into Balanchine's company. Balanchine had at his command an excellent corps of dancers, headed by Anatole Vilzak and William Dollar, and including such accomplished artists as Leda Anchutina, Gisella Caccialanza, Eugene Loring, Kathryn Mullowney, Lew and Harold Christensen, Ruthanna Boris, Ruby Asquith, Annabelle Lyon, Albia Kavan, Douglas Coudy, Elise Reiman and others who have since made their mark. However, his approach to opera ballet was so startlingly unconventional that the staid subscribers of the horseshoe (no longer "diamond," to be sure) were shocked as they had never been by the former company's placid routines. On the reduced-rate Sunday night concert programs (to which the influential box-holders never came) Balanchine presented some of his loveliest ballets, such as *Serenade, Mozartiana*, and *Reminiscence*, as well as William Dollar's first choreographic work, the Chopin *Concerto*, later revised as the *Constantia* which is danced today. For the popular-priced spring season of 1936, equally ignored by the subscribers with well-lined purses, he created a delightful new work, *The Bat*. He also managed to stir up considerable controversy with a new version of Gluck's *Orfeo*, designed by Pavel Tchelitchew and mimed by Daphne Vance, Lew Christensen and William Dollar, with the singers remaining in the pit. Perhaps today, after fourteen years, the public would be ready for a revival of this extraordinary production, which was either violently hated or violently admired by all who saw it.

Balanchine found it increasingly difficult to confine his very original talents within the framework of opera. In 1938 his *Apollo*, introduced as a curtain-raiser for *Salome*, passed almost unnoticed; it had to wait several more years, until it was revived by Ballet Theatre, before it was fully appreciated here. After three years of hectic and sometimes exciting struggle Balanchine and his group withdrew, and the Metropolitan once more formed its own ballet company.

For the position of choreographer Johnson chose Boris Romanoff, a graduate, like Balanchine, of the Russian Ballet, but a man whose wide experience had included many years in the leading opera houses of Europe and South America. The leading dancers were Felia Doubrovska, formerly of the Diaghilev company, Ruth Chanova, a young American whose promising career was cut short by her early death, a few years later, and Maria Gambarelli, who had begun her career as a student in the Metropolitan Ballet School some years before. Outstanding in Romanoff's first season was his beautiful production of *Orfeo*, in which he directed much of the stage action of the singers as well as the dancers, and achieved a rare and memorable harmony between movement and music. Doubrovska gave an unforgettable interpretation of the Unhappy Spirit.

The Metropolitan still had no provisions for new ballets in its economy budget. (Balanchine's independent productions had been subsidized by

Warburg and Kirstein.) Without any allotment for settings or costumes, Romanoff managed to present a Handel ballet, *Spirits' Revelry,* and a version of the Walpurgis Night Ballet which, however, was never given in connection with *Faust,* but only at concerts, a special ballet demonstration, and similar occasions. Romanoff was fortunate in the acquisition, after his first season, of Ruthanna Boris as prima ballerina. When she left to join the Ballet Russe de Monte Carlo she was replaced by Marina Svetlova, a former soloist of the Original Ballet Russe. Romanoff's regime lasted (with the exception of an interlude when Laurent Novikoff, former partner of Pavlova, was choreographer) until 1950, when he resigned to go to Italy as principal choreographer at La Scala. Under his direction a number of fine soloists, such as Monna Montez, Aida Alvarez, Irene Hawthorne, Nina Youshkevitch, George Chaffee, Grant Mouradoff, Leon Varkas, Beatrice Weinberger, Audrey Keene, and others appeared in the opera ballets; but their opportunities were hindered by the limitations of opera and the lack of any separate ballets in which to demonstrate their abilities.

In 1950 the Metropolitan Opera Ballet was reorganized again, under Ballet Theatre, with a distinguished choreographer, Antony Tudor, at its head. Although the ballet was to appear in the 1950/51 season in comparatively few operas, its assignments in two of them, *Die Fledermaus* and *Faust,* were of considerable importance. It had a ready-made outlet, the Ballet Theatre company, for those dancers who might outgrow the opera frame. The Metropolitan could still provide a sympathetic atmosphere for the education and development of young dance artists, and a new chapter in its history was to begin.

—*Dance,* January 1951.

Appendix

Footnotes to article V, *New York's First Ballet Season, 1792:*

[1] George C. D. Odell, *Annals of the New York Stage* (New York 1927) I 21.

[2] *Virginia Gazette,* Williamsburg, Oct 3, 1751.

[3] *Rivington's Gazeteer,* New York, May 19, 1774 (Odell I 181).

[4] Odell I 228.

[5] Record of Deaths, Vol. I. New York City Department of Health. The entry for Placide states that he was born in Paris and died in New York City on July 26, 1812, aged 62 years. The record of Placide's death was unearthed by Mme. Sylvie Chevalley, who kindly called it to my attention.

[6] Émile Campardon, *Les Comédiens du Roi de la Troupe Italienne* (Paris 1880) 73—81. For Mme. Billioni's obituary, see *Almanache des Spectacles de Paris* XXX (Paris 1783) 17—19.

[7] *Almanach* XXI (Paris 1772) 13.

[8] E. D. de Manne and C. Ménétrier, *Galerie Historique des Comédiens de la Troupe de Nicolet* (Lyon 1869) 8, 16—20.

[9] Richard Findlater, *Grimaldi, King of Clowns* (London 1955) 19.

[10] Émile Campardon, *Les Spectacles de la Foire* (Paris 1877) II 136.

[11] Jean Fouchard, *Artistes et Repertoire des Scènes de Saint-Domingue* (Port-au-Prince 1955) 70—71, 248, 267.

[12] The death record of Dama Suzanne Théodore Vaillande, widow of Louis Douvillier, at St. Louis Cathedral, New Orleans, states that she died August 30, 1826, at the age of 48; that she was a native of Dole, France, educated in Paris. It is possible that she may be identified as the Marie Anne, illegitimate daughter of Marie Reine Vailland [sic] of Dole, who was born there on September 28, 1778. (Letter from J. Hézard, Consérvateur des Archives, Mairie de Dole, to Lillian Moore, Sept 11, 1955.)

[13] Oscar George Theodore Sonneck, *Catalogue of Opera Librettos published before 1800* (Washington, D.C. 1914) I 1111.

[14] Antoine d'Origny, *Annales du Théâtre Italien* (Paris 1788) I 292.

[15] Sonneck I 265.

[16] Alfonso Joseph Sheafe, "Dictionary of the Dance" (MS in the Dance Collection of The New York Public Library) XL 6930.

[17] New York *Daily Advertiser* Feb 3, 1792. — Hereafter abbreviated as *Adv* (all dates cited from this paper are 1792).

[18] *Adv* Feb 6.

[19] *New York Journal and Patriotic Register* Feb 8, 1792.

[20] *Journal de Paris*, Nov 5 and 19, 1785.

[21] Charles Dickens, *Memoirs of Joseph Grimaldi* (London 1853) 10.

[22] *Indice de' Spettacoli Teatrali*, 1774—75 (Milan 1775) 71.

[23] Ivor Guest, *The Romantic Ballet in England* (London 1954) 147, 149, 150, 164.

[24] *Indice de' Spettacoli Teatrali*, 1781—82 (Milan 1782) 56.

[25] Campardon, *Les Spectacles de la Foire* II 303.

[26] De Manne and Ménétrier 17.

[27] (François Maire Mayeur de Saint-Paul), *Le Chroniqueur Désoeuvré, ou l'Espion du Boulevard du Temple* (Londres 1782) 152—153.

[28] Wilson Disher, *Clowns and Pantomimes* (London 1925) 144.

[29] *South Carolina State Gazette* (Charleston) Feb 19, 1796.

[30] Playbill, John St. Theatre, New York, Apr 24, 1792 (Harvard Theatre Collection).

[31] *South Carolina State Gazette* May 27, 1794.

[32] Anonymous article, "The Charleston Stage Sixty Years Ago," from an unidentified newspaper, in Scrapbook MWEX x n.c. 703, p 138, Theatre Collection, The New York Public Library.

[33] *A History of the American Theatre* (New York 1832) 289.

[34] *Dramatic Life as I Found It* (St. Louis 1880) 146—147.

[35] De Manne and Ménétrier 17.

[36] *New-York Journal and Patriotic Register*, Feb 29.

[37] Alfred Loewenberg, *Annals of Opera, 1597-1940* (Geneva 1955) 446.

[38] Playbill, John St. Theatre, New York, Mar 26, 1792 (Harvard Theatre Collection).

[39] Playbill, John St. Theatre, New York, Apr 18, 1792 (Harvard Theatre Collection).

[40] Thomas Clark Pollock, *The Philadelphia Theatre in the Eighteenth Century* (Philadelphia 1933) 168.

[41] *New-York Journal and Patriotic Register*, May 3. (The title of the pantomime is actually spelled here, *Harlequin Baloonist, or, Perrot in the Clouds.*)

[42] William W. Clapp, Jr, *A Record of the Boston Stage* (Boston 1853) 7.

[43] Eola Willis, *The Charleston Stage in the XVIII Century* (Columbia, S. C. 1924); W. Stanley Holle, *The Ante-Bellum Charleston Theatre* (Tuscaloosa, Ala. 1946).

[44] Charles William Janson, *The Stranger in America, 1793—1806*, ed Dr. Carl S. Driver from the London edition of 1807 (New York 1935) 369—370.

[45] See note 12.

[46] T. Allston Brown, *History of the American Stage* (New York 1870) 237.

[47] See Elizabeth Clarke Kieffer, "John Durang, The First Native American Dancer," *The Dutchman* VI (Lancaster, June 1954) 26—38, and Lillian Moore, "John Durang, the First American Dancer," *Dance Index* I no. 8 (New York, August 1942). The latter monograph was reprinted in *Chronicles of the American Dance*, ed. Paul Magriel (New York 1948).

Index

Index